Practical Veneering

Practical Veneering

Charles H. Hayward

Sterling Publishing Co., Inc. New York

Published in 1979 by
Sterling Publishing Co., Inc.
Two Park Avenue
New York, N.Y. 10016

ISBN 0-8069-8876-2
Previously
ISBN 0-237-44812-2

Printed in U.S.A.

Contents

Woodworkers' Conversion Tables

Imperial inches	Metric millimetres	Woodworkers' parlance (mm.)	Metric millimetres	Imperial inches	Woodworkers' parlance (in.)
$\frac{1}{32}$	0·8	1 bare	1	0·039	$\frac{1}{16}$ bare
$\frac{1}{16}$	1·6	$1\frac{1}{2}$	2	0·078	$\frac{1}{16}$ full
$\frac{1}{8}$	3·2	3 full	3	0·118	$\frac{1}{8}$ bare
$\frac{3}{16}$	4·8	5 bare	4	0·157	$\frac{5}{32}$
$\frac{1}{4}$	6·4	$6\frac{1}{2}$	5	0·196	$\frac{3}{16}$ full
$\frac{5}{16}$	7·9	8 bare	6	0·236	$\frac{1}{4}$ bare
$\frac{3}{8}$	9·5	$9\frac{1}{2}$	7	0·275	$\frac{1}{4}$ full
$\frac{7}{16}$	11·1	11 full	8	0·314	$\frac{5}{16}$
$\frac{1}{2}$	12·7	$12\frac{1}{2}$ full	9	0·353	$\frac{3}{8}$ bare
$\frac{9}{16}$	14·3	$14\frac{1}{2}$ bare	10	0·393	$\frac{3}{8}$ full
$\frac{5}{8}$	15·9	16 bare	20	0·787	$\frac{13}{16}$ bare
$\frac{11}{16}$	17·5	$17\frac{1}{2}$	30	1·181	$1\frac{3}{16}$
$\frac{3}{4}$	19·1	19 full	40	1·574	$1\frac{9}{16}$ full
$\frac{13}{16}$	20·6	$20\frac{1}{2}$	50	1·968	$1\frac{15}{16}$ full
$\frac{7}{8}$	22·2	22 full	60	2·362	$2\frac{3}{8}$ bare
$\frac{15}{16}$	23·8	24 bare	70	2·755	$2\frac{3}{4}$
1	25·4	$25\frac{1}{2}$	80	3·148	$3\frac{1}{8}$ full
2	50·8	51 bare	90	3·542	$3\frac{9}{16}$ bare
3	76·2	76 full	100	3·936	$3\frac{15}{16}$
4	101·4	$101\frac{1}{2}$	150	5·904	$5\frac{15}{16}$ bare
5	127·0	127	200	7·872	$7\frac{7}{8}$
6	152·4	$152\frac{1}{2}$	300	11·808	$11\frac{13}{16}$
7	177·5	178 bare	400	15·744	$15\frac{3}{4}$
8	203·2	203 full	500	19·680	$19\frac{11}{16}$
9	228·6	$228\frac{1}{2}$	600	23·616	$23\frac{5}{8}$ bare
10	254·0	254	700	27·552	$27\frac{9}{16}$
11	279·5	$279\frac{1}{2}$	800	31·488	$31\frac{1}{2}$
12	304·8	305 bare	900	35·424	$35\frac{7}{16}$
18	457·2	457 full	1,000	39·360	$39\frac{3}{8}$ bare
24	609·6	$609\frac{1}{2}$			
36	914·4	$914\frac{1}{2}$			

Note
The imperial and metric sizes given for tools and joint parts etc. cannot work out exact, but providing one works to one or the other there is no difficulty. In the timber trade it is accepted that 1 in. = 25 mm.

Introduction

The purpose of veneering

There is an old illusion that the term veneering is synonymous with woodwork which is cheap and shoddy; that it represents an attempt to cover up cheap materials and poor workmanship; and that it is altogether inferior to solid wood. Nothing could be farther from the truth. Properly completed, a piece of veneered woodwork is as reliable as a solid job. It is made of the best timber, calls for the highest quality workmanship, and is anything but a cheap process to carry out. That veneering *has* been made use of to cover a nailed-up carcase must be admitted, but this is merely the abuse of a craft which has its definite uses and advantages

The chief advantage of veneering is that it enables effects to be obtained which would be impossible or at any rate very unreliable if carried out in solid wood. For instance, there are certain woods which, although beautiful in figure, are liable to twist and split if used in the solid because of their wild grain. In addition, they seldom have much strength owing to the short grain, which in parts may run practically at right angles through the wood. It is obvious then that veneering provides the only means by which such woods can be used, since by fixing them in thin sheets to a groundwork made of plain but reliable timber, the necessary strength is provided. Then again, consider the fine effect produced by built-up patterns and the introduction of various kinds of woods in one panel. A little reflection shows that such work would be out of the question in solid wood. Apart from any lack of strength and constructional difficulty, there would be inevitable trouble due to shrinkage. In addition there is the question of shaped work. Within certain limits this can be done in solid wood, but if the degree of curvature is great, either the work will lack strength because of the short grain, or the surface will show a number of joints contrived in an endeavour to provide strength. By using veneer the job can be built up in a convenient way which will provide maximum strength, and it will show a fine grain in every part and be free from visible joints.

Apart from the foregoing, however, veneering has become a necessity today partly because of the ever-growing scarcity of finely-figured solid woods, and also the short supply of solid timber suitable for the ground work. Although the latter is not seen in the finished product it must be sound and reliable. Consequently man-made materials such as plywood, blockboard, and chipboard have usually to be used. They have their advantages too in that they are available in almost unlimited widths, and if of good quality are reliable. Set against this is the fact that the edges have to be lipped (unless used purely as panels) to conceal the layers, or to enable mouldings to be worked.

The writer would like to express his gratitude to the many firms who have supplied photographs of veneered work or machines used in veneering, given information on adhesives or special branches of veneering, and in particular to F. R. Shadbolt & Sons Ltd., for their help in demonstrating modern methods of factory production. Special thanks are due to Mr. A. Cooper for his assistance regarding correction of faults in veneer leaves, and the procedure in making built-up designs.

Chapter one

The processes in brief

To make a broad division there are two ways in which veneering can be done; by press or by hand methods. These again can be subdivided as follows.

Presses
1. Hydraulic thermostatically-controlled multiplate machine presses, or short-cycle continuous presses. Used for panels, table tops, etc.
2. Compressed air or vacuum presses with rubber sheet or bag. Used mostly for shaped work.
3. Hand presses, screw controlled. Used mostly for flat panels but can be adapted for shaped work with formers.

Hand methods
1. Caul veneering;
2. Hammer veneering;
3. Special contact adhesive method.

Presses

This is the most commonly used today, at any rate in the trade. The reason is partly one of

Fig. 1A (below) Rosewood sideboard; drawer fronts and cupboard doors were veneered together then cut through to form the separate parts, giving perfect grain pattern. Designed by Martin Hall MSIA. Photograph by courtesy of Gordon Russell Ltd.

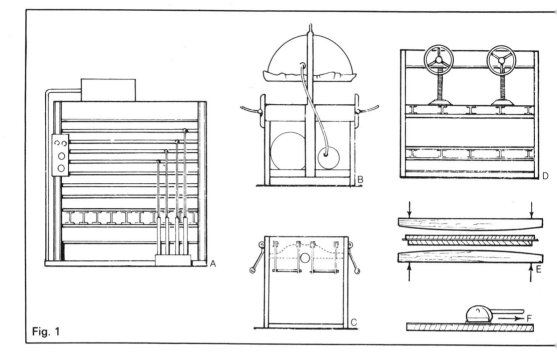

Fig. 1

Fig. 1 Diagrams illustrating the chief methods of veneering. A multi-plate hydraulic press; B compressed air press; C vacuum press; D screw operated press; E caul with cross-bearers; F pressing down veneer with veneering hammer.

economics, and partly the availability of modern adhesives which have several advantages over the traditional animal or casein glues. The days when a small cabinet-making workshop carried out all branches of the craft including veneering have largely passed because it would not pay a man to install a press which would come in for only occasional use. It is cheaper to give out the work to a firm specializing in such work. In the case of a large factory it is a different matter because the press would be in constant use and would soon pay for its cost, though even here it is usual for veneer to be laid in just one section of the factory which specializes in such work and nothing else.

On the question of adhesives most present day glues need a press or at least the hand method equivalent of a caul. The older hammer method

(see page 57) cannot be used. Their advantage i that many of them are extremely damp- an heat-resistant and strong, making them ideal fc such purposes as table tops etc. It is true tha many table tops in the past were veneered, bu generally thick saw-cut veneer was used, thoug even here the glue in the long run was liable t fail, resulting in bubbles being formed (in th veneer), possibly the result of a hot dish bein stood on the surface, or the consequence c exposure to damp.

Another point about some modern adhesives i that, although they may be used cold, they can b heat cured. The benefit of this is that a thermo statically controlled multi-plate press can be use in which plates can be flooded with hot wate after the insertion of the veneered panels, enablin the latter to be removed after about 10 minutes leaving the press free for another batch of panels Alternatively the work may be passed through short-cycle continuous press in which the ad hesive is quickly cured.

Screw presses, although not so widely used a

formerly, are still useful for some work, and particularly for one-off jobs, or when curved formers or cauls for shaped work are to be used. For the latter, however, either the vacuum or the compressed air press (when available) is the more generally useful.

Hand methods

Caul Veneering. In this a flat panel of wood (sometimes faced with zinc) is cramped down over the veneer with a sheet of newspaper interposed to prevent any squeezed-out glue from sticking to it. When animal glue is used, the caul is thoroughly heated beforehand so that the glue is re-liquefied and is pressed out, enabling the veneer to make close contact with the groundwork. In the case of large panels the cramps are applied over pairs of curved cross-bearers so that pressure is felt at the centre first, forcing surplus glue out at the edges. Any jointing in the veneer is done beforehand, the parts being held together with gummed tape.

Hammer veneering. Both groundwork and veneer having been glued, the latter is placed in position and smoothed down with the hands. About one half of the surface is lightly dampened and a warm flat-iron passed over it so that the glue beneath is made runny. A tool known as a veneering hammer is pressed over the surface zigzag fashion so that the veneer is pressed down into close contact with the groundwork and surplus glue is squeezed out. The remaining half is then treated in the same way. When jointing is needed the veneers are laid with a slight overlap and a chisel-cut made through both. The waste strips are peeled away and a piece of gummed tape stuck over the joint to prevent it from opening as the moisture dries out.

Contact adhesive. This is used mostly for small work, and sometimes for certain shaped work where it would be difficult or impossible to apply a shaped caul. The adhesive is applied to both groundwork and veneer and allowed to become touch dry. When placed in position the grab is immediate so that careful positioning is essential, though some adhesives allow for slight movement for a short while. Either a roller or the veneering hammer is used to press down the veneer.

The choice of method is thus one of individual circumstances. So far as the small workshop is concerned, however, there is one important consideration when large work has to be done. The use of a press large enough would probably be out of the question, which leaves only the choice of caul or hammer veneering. The former requires a caul slightly larger than the work and needs pairs of curved cross-bearers and a large number of cramps or handscrews. If that is impracticable only hammer veneering remains, for which reason this method is still favoured in the small workshop.

Chapter two

Groundwork

Whatever the method used for laying the veneer, the use of the right material for the groundwork and its correct preparation are of the utmost importance, because it is upon these that the success of the work largely depends. It is more or less impossible to produce a good result if the groundwork is faulty. Any blemish in it will have its effect upon the veneer in the long run. The work may appear successful when first completed, but time is one of the most important tests of veneering, and it is only after an interval of a year or so that its success is finally determined.

How veneer pulls. The first point to realize is that veneering has certain peculiarities, chief amongst which is its liability to pull the work hollow as it dries out. Thin boards suffer more in this respect than thick ones, but even a board of 25mm. (1in.) or more in thickness may pull out of shape unless it is held rigidly (like a carcase end, for instance) or unless special precautions are taken.

The cause of this pull is the moisture that may be used in the process and in the glue. When the

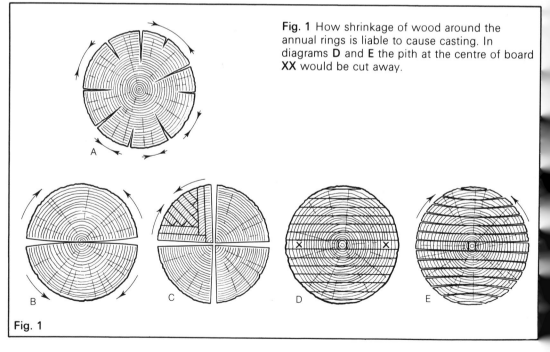

Fig. 1 How shrinkage of wood around the annual rings is liable to cause casting. In diagrams **D** and **E** the pith at the centre of board **XX** would be cut away.

Fig. 1

latter is applied to the veneer it causes the veneer to swell, and the same thing happens when it is brushed on to the groundwork. In the case of the hammer method, the veneer has to be dampened after being placed in position, causing still more swelling. Heat from the flat-iron makes the veneer pliable due to the generation of steam, and when the veneering hammer is used it may stretch the veneer. As the moisture dries out the swelling and stretching are reversed, and as the glue has now exerted its grip the veneer pulls the ground-work hollow.

With great care, avoiding unnecessary moisture and heat, and not stretching the veneer, much of this casting can be avoided. In fact, some skilled craftsmen are able to prevent it altogether. This is dealt with more fully in Chapter seven, Hammer veneering, but it is something which has to be taken into account, and it is safe to say that few men could successfully veneer a panel, say, 12mm. ($\frac{1}{2}$in.) or less in thickness on one side only by the hammer method without its pulling hollow on drying out.

One way of minimising the risk when solid wood is used for the groundwork is to lay the veneer on the heart side of the wood, because the pull of the veneer is then opposed to the natural twisting tendency of the wood itself. Fig. 1, A and B shows a section through a log, and the direction in which the boards are liable to twist is clearly indicated at E. If, therefore, the wood is veneered on the heart side, the pull of the veneer will to a certain extent be counteracted. This is shown in Fig. 2, A and B. Thus, when a carcase having veneered ends and top has to be made, it is a safeguard to have the heart side outwards. It is simple to tell the heart side by examining the end grain. If the curve of the annual rings is imagined to be continued round as in Fig. 3, it is obvious which side is nearer the heart.

The best safeguard, however (and it is essential in an unsupported piece of work such as a flush door), is to veneer both sides and to select a groundwork which is free from any tendency to twist. If Fig. 1D is examined, it will be seen that the board XX is in line with the centre or heart. In other words, it is cut radially from the log, and is not liable to twist one way or the other. The reason for this is that a log shrinks for the greater

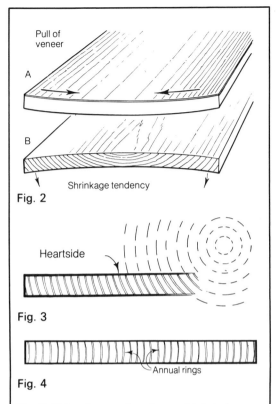

Fig. 2

Pull of veneer

A

B

Shrinkage tendency

Heartside

Fig. 3

Annual rings

Fig. 4

Fig. 2 Side of groundwork on which to lay veneer. By putting veneer on heart side the pull is opposed to the natural twisting tendency.

Fig. 3 How to tell heart side of board. The lines show continuation of annual rings.

Fig. 4 Quarter-cut board used as a groundwork.

part around the annual rings, and, since these rings pass through a radially cut board more or less at right angles, the only effect of shrinkage is slightly to reduce its thickness, and this is so small as not to matter—in any case, most shrinkage will have taken place during seasoning. Thus the board XX, Fig. 1D, should stand well if veneered on both sides. Note that the actual pith or centre is cut away and is not used. Fig. 4 shows a radially cut board. The same thickness of veneer must be used on both sides as otherwise the thicker will exert a greater pull than the other.

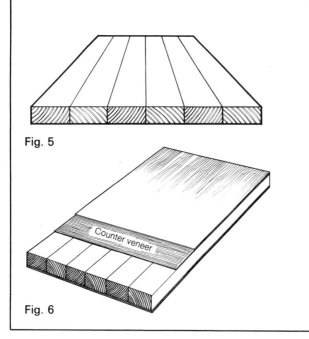

Fig. 5

Counter veneer

Fig. 6

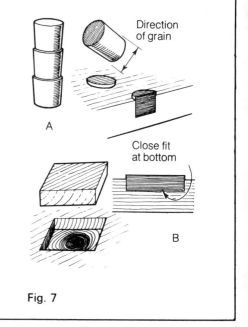

Direction of grain

A

Close fit at bottom

B

Fig. 7

Fig. 5 Ground built up of strips of straight-grained wood. Note that the heart sides are alternately up and down.

Fig. 6 Similar groundwork to that above but this has been counter-veneered both sides.

Fig. 7 Filling in blemishes. **A** shows pellets suitable for small places such as screw holes. For larger holes plugs are used, **B**.

Special forms of groundworks. However, it is not always practicable to use radially cut boards, and another reliable method is to joint up a series of strips with the heart side alternately up and down, as in Fig. 5. In this way any twisting tendency in one board is counteracted by that of the next, which tends to twist in the opposite direction. Yet another plan is to clamp the panel, though it is essential that perfectly seasoned wood is used, because otherwise the main panel is liable to split in the event of shrinkage owing to its being held rigidly. Whatever type of groundwork is used, however, well-seasoned wood is essential.

The most satisfactory system when solid wood is used is to counter-veneer, that is double-veneer both sides, the undersheets having the grain at right angles with that of the groundwork. The face veneers have their grain in the same directions as

the groundwork as shown in Fig. 6. It is expensive and is done only in the best work, but for an important job it is worth the extra cost. The cross-veneers can be plain, since they do not show. See also page 21.

Woods to use. An excellent wood for a groundwork is yellow pine, though it is expensive and very rare nowadays. Sometimes, however, old timber from a dismantled item can be found. In common with other softwoods it is liable to soak up more than its share of the glue, and it should therefore be sized to seal the pores before the veneer is laid. Baltic pine is often used as a groundwork but it should be as free as possible of knots. If there are any, these should be chopped out and filled. Fig. 7. shows how this is done. Sometimes a diamond-shaped filling is suitable. The plugs are allowed to stand proud and are levelled after the

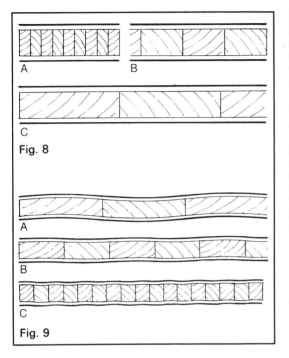

Fig. 8

Fig. 9

Fig. 8 Laminated, block, and batten boards. In laminated board **A** the core strips should not exceed 7mm. ($\frac{9}{32}$in.) in thickness. Block board core blocks **B** are not more than 25mm. (1in.) wide. The core battens of batten board **C** are not over 75mm. (3in.) wide.

Fig. 9 Potential warping of laminated boards. **A** batten board; **B** block board; **C** lamin board.

glue has set. When pellets are used it is essential that the grain runs crosswise as shown. Dowels are entirely unsuitable, as the grain runs lengthwise and would remain standing proud of the surface in the event of the wood of the groundwork shrinking.

It will be realized that, although a knot may be levelled perfectly when cleaned up, it is liable to show later because its grain runs through the thickness of the wood, and whilst the surrounding wood shrinks in its thickness, the knot is left standing up. Another danger is that, as it shrinks, it necessarily reduces its diameter and may eventually drop right out. Small indentations can be filled in with plaster of Paris, this being mixed with thin glue and allowed to harden thoroughly before cleaning off. If the depression is shallow it should be well roughened to afford a key. Better still, avoid such blemishes altogether.

Oak is not the most satisfactory of woods, though sometimes it has to be used. Reproductions of period pieces often necessitate its use. Its disadvantage is that it is somewhat coarse in the

grain, and if laid with thin veneer, after a period of time, the pattern of the grain can sometimes be seen right through to the surface. Another point is that a radially cut board necessarily shows the figured rays on its surface, and, as these are harder than the rest of the wood, they are liable to stand up and show through to the surface. This means that plain boards have to be used which are more liable to twist. It is important if such a board is veneered on one side only that the veneer is laid on the heart side.

Whitewood makes a successful groundwork if reliable stuff is chosen. Gummy woods such as pitch pine are unsuitable. Other woods that can be used successfully are birch, beech (avoid quarter-cut figured boards if you are using thin veneer), American whitewood, obeche, and so on; but it is largely a question of its soundness and whether it has been seasoned. At all costs avoid green timber; it is not only liable to twist and split, but the dampness in it will have a deteriorating effect upon the glue.

Laminated board and plywood. Apart from solid wood, there are various manufactured substances which are excellent for a groundwork. Of these, laminated board is most satisfactory. Its advantage is that it is perfectly flat and is not liable to shrink. It is made up of a centre core consisting of seasoned, narrow strips placed side by side, with a facing at each side, the grain of which runs at right angles with that of the core. This is shown at Fig. 8A. In common with solid woods, however, it is liable to pull hollow if veneered on one side only. Unsupported work must therefore be veneered on both sides. For the best work a cross-veneer can be laid at each side, but this is not so necessary as in solid wood because the facings of the board itself serve the purpose. It is advisable to put the grain of the veneer at right angles with that of the facings.

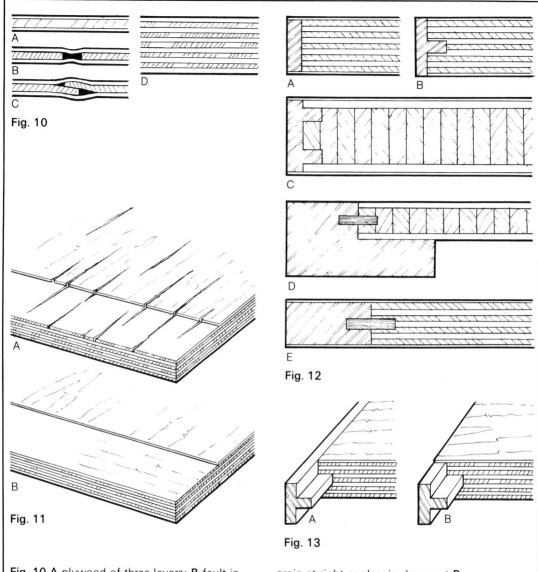

Fig. 10

Fig. 11

Fig. 12

Fig. 13

Fig. 10 A plywood of three layers; **B** fault in plywood due to gap in centre layer; **C** ridge caused by overlap; **D** multi-ply.

Fig. 11 Possible cause of cracking when veneering plywood. At **A** the grain of the veneer is in the same direction as surface of plywood, hence the splits. The correct way, with the grain at right angles, is shown at **B**.

Fig. 12 Alternative forms of lipping for plywood and lamin board.

Fig. 13 Alternatives of applying lipping after or before veneering. It is largely a question of the use to which the work is to be put.

Block board is made on a similar principle, but the core strips are wider. It does not make so satisfactory a groundwork. The same thing applies to batten board, in which the strips are still wider. The three boards are shown in Fig. 8, and the following are the maximum widths of the core strips:

Lamin board, 7mm. $(\frac{9}{32}$in.$)$
Block board, 25mm. (1in.)
Batten board, 75mm. (3in.)

The reason for the superiority of the board with narrow core strips is made clear in Fig. 9. It is obvious that the wider the strips the greater the potential warping. The warping tendency of wide strips—a series of wide waves, is shown in exaggeration at A. At B this is reduced considerably, the waves being much smaller owing to the narrower strips. At C they have practically disappeared. Of course warping would not occur to the extent shown, especially when faced with the outer layers, but the writer has seen a large veneered door made from block board in which the waves could be easily seen owing to the high polish. To minimise the risk of corrugation the lamin board should be stacked as long as possible after being received from the manufacturers. The surface is then smoothed with coarse glasspaper held on a flat block and dusted.

Plywood too is used extensively for veneering, but it is essential that it be the best quality. A cheap commercial make is worse than useless because the layers themselves are liable to separate and there are usually knots. Furthermore, it is seldom flat, and depressions are liable to develop owing to gaps in the joints in the centre layer. The gap may be filled with glue or cement, and as this dries out and shrinks the top layer is pulled in and the veneer is pulled with it. This is shown at Fig. 10B. Gaboon multi-ply makes an excellent groundwork, especially for flush doors which have to be self-supporting.

It is imperative that all plywood should have the veneer laid with its grain at right angles with that of the surface of the ply. The reason is that, although the job may look all right when first done, after a month or two a number of cracks may develop, and there is no satisfactory way of putting things right. The cause of this cracking is that, as the veneer shrinks, it pulls the outer layer of the ply with it, and this, having been rotary cut,

has not much strength across the grain—indeed, it may already have minor cracks which open out under the pull of the veneer. The ply thus splits and the veneer opens with it as at Fig. 11A.

If, however, the grain of the veneer runs at right angles with that of the groundwork, as at B, it can resist the pull, and the veneer merely stretches equally all over instead of developing cracks. The same thing applies to lamin board. The only other plan is to cross-veneer the panel first and put the final veneer over this; if expense is not important it is an excellent method.

A feature common to both laminated board and plywood is that the edges are bound to show the thicknesses of which they are built up. It is not practicable to veneer these edges because the end grain will not grip the glue well. Consequently it is necessary to add edgings all round. A few methods of applying lippings are given in Fig. 12. In the simplest way, A, a thin strip is glued on, levelled, and the surface veneered afterwards. A better and stronger lipping is that at B in which the board is grooved to take a tongue. For a thick board two tongues could be arranged, as at C. D shows a lipping useful when the edge requires thicknessing. All of them can be used for either plywood or laminated board. Those who have only hand methods will find the T form of edging awkward to make, and the type at E has its advantage in that it is simple to work the groove in both pieces and insert a loose tongue.

A point to consider is whether the lipping is to be applied before or after veneering. If fixed first it is entirely concealed by the veneer, and this may be essential in some circumstances. On the other hand, if the lipping is added after veneering it is bound to be visible. At the same time it will protect the edge of the veneer, and it should be remembered that the edges are always the most vulnerable part. For work exposed to hard wear, then, it would be better to veneer first and fix the lipping afterwards. The two ideas are shown in Fig. 13.

Preparation of groundwork. It is assumed that the reader knows how to clean up and true a surface. A panel plane should be used to ensure its being not only true in length and width but also free from winding. A pair of winding strips, used

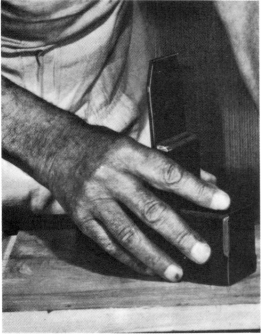

Fig. 14 (above) Testing groundwork with winding strips.

Fig. 15 (left) Using toothing plane on groundwork. It is worked in all directions to take out inequalities and roughen the surface.

as in Fig. 14, is an excellent test in this connection. The plane, however, is bound to leave marks, and to get rid of these a toothing plane is used, as in Fig. 15. In appearance this is somewhat similar to a smoothing plane, but the cutter is practically vertical, and has a series of grooves in it which produce a number of fine points at the cutting edge rather like the teeth of a fine saw (Fig. 16). When being sharpened, only the bevel is worked on the stone. The back is not touched, because this would flatten out the ridges.

It is worked across the surface of the groundwork in all directions as shown in Fig. 15, so that any 'waves' left by the plane are taken out. Care must be taken that the edges are not dubbed over. The whole surface in this way will be scored all

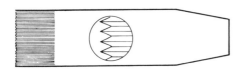

Fig. 16

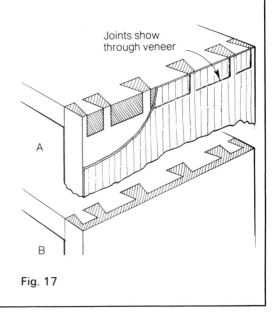

Joints show through veneer

A

B

Fig. 17

Fig. 16 Toothing plane cutter. The back has a series of grooves so that when sharpened there is a saw-like cutting edge.

Fig. 17 Corner of dovetailed cabinet with veneered ends. The through dovetail at **A** is liable to show through to the surface after a while. It is therefore better to use the lapped dovetail at **B**.

over and this provides an excellent key for the glue. The hand should be passed lightly over the work in all directions afterwards, when any waves will be easily detected. Testing with the straight-edge is not necessary, because it is assumed that the preliminary planing has made the board flat and true. Every part of the surface must be scored because, apart from providing a key, it reveals the truth of the work. The plane reduces the high parts and rides over any depressions. Thus, if any portions are left without scores, it suggests these are low and that the surrounding wood needs reducing.

Finally, all dust should be brushed off because this might cause small lumps beneath the veneer. As already mentioned, softwood must be sized to seal the pores. Ordinary Scotch glue well thinned with water can be used when this adhesive is being applied for the veneering. For resin glue use the latter thinned out with water as a size. When dry it is lightly rubbed down with coarse glass-paper to remove undue roughness and dusted.

Dealing with end grain. It is difficult to veneer end grain successfully because it does not hold the glue well, but the process is sometimes un-avoidable. It should be well sized first, about three coats being given, each being allowed to dry out before the next is applied.

When possible, veneering over elaborate joints such as dovetails should be avoided, because owing to shrinkage they are liable to show through to the surface, as shown in Fig. 17A. If it cannot be helped (it usually can be avoided by cutting special joints to suit) a thick veneer should be laid. In the old days very thick veneers were often used, so thick that they often amounted to facings, and these could be laid over such joints successfully. A thin veneer, however, will inevitably pull to the shape of the groundwork.

Cross- or counter-veneering. As explained on pages 16 and 22, this makes a reliable job and is specially suitable for panels which are not directly fixed to adjoining parts and rely purely on their own construction to keep them flat—flush doors, for example. Both sides should be treated alike with veneers of the same thickness, and if a

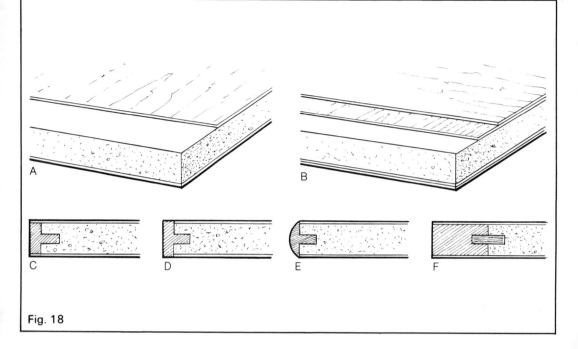

Fig. 18

Fig. 18 Chipboard used as a groundwork for veneer. **A** veneered both sides; **B** counter-veneered; **C** lipped before veneering; **D** lipped after veneering; **E** rounded lipping; **F** lipped with loose tongue.

pattern such as quartering is used on the front, the back should have a similar if simplified version. It is advisable to finish off each panel independently. For instance, when several panels have to be veneered, the back and front of each should be dealt with at the same time rather than first laying the back of each, then all the fronts. One side should be veneered immediately after the other. Do not lay the front one day and the back another.

The hammer, caul or press can be used. In the first case, having laid the counter-veneers, allow them to harden, then lightly tooth flat. The face veneers follow. Avoid too much heat and dampness so that the counter-veneers are not disturbed. When the caul is used the usual plan is to lay both counter-veneers in one operation, using two cauls. Face veneers follow in the same way after tooth-

ing, but avoid using any grease on the sole of the plane. It is possible to lay all four veneers together, but only when there are no joints in the counter-veneers.

Chipboard. This is frequently used as a ground-work for veneering, and the general notes on treating both sides alike apply, Fig. 18A. One point to note is that some varieties have coarser chips on one side than the other, and the finer side should be the face side. For best results the panel should be counter-veneered, the outer veneer at right angles with that beneath (B).

Both surfaces of the chipboard should be sanded with coarse grade before veneering, and the dust should be got rid of before gluing.

Lipping is usually necessary, partly to conceal the exposed edges, and also to prevent wear—in some cases it may be needed to give a fixing for fittings such as hinges. At Fig. 18C, the lipping is fixed first and is entirely concealed. If added after veneering (D) it necessarily shows but has the advantage of protecting the veneered edges

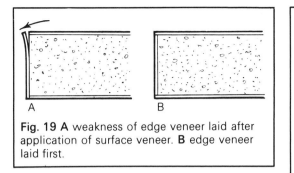

Fig. 19 A weakness of edge veneer laid after application of surface veneer. **B** edge veneer laid first.

which are always liable to damage. In some work such as table tops the rounded edging at E has the advantage that it both protects the veneer edges and does not show at the top.

Ready-veneered chipboard panels are widely used, these having the edges veneered as well as the surfaces. These edge veneers are added afterwards, and, although satisfactory for some work, are liable to be pulled off if used for a table top as at Fig. 19A. Objects drawn across the edges are liable to force the edge veneers off. If used for such a purpose it would be more satisfactory to add lipping at Fig. 18, D or E, the edge veneers being stripped off first. For the man who lays the veneers himself it would be more satisfactory to veneer the edges first as at Fig. 19B or, better still, use the lipping as at Fig. 18C. As all three

Fig. 19A (above) Corner cabinet in English burr walnut, interior lined with bleached sapelewood and mahogany curls. By Ernest Joyce MSIA.

lippings Fig. 18 C, D, and E, are awkward to make by hand, tongued lipping F can be an advantage.

Chapter three

Kinds of veneers and veneer timbers

Apart from the woods used and the individual varieties of each, veneers are known by the method used in cutting them. There are several ways in which this is done: flat slicing, rotary cutting, and half-rotary slicing, each of which has its own particular purpose and peculiarities. Originally veneers were also sawn on a huge circular saw, and were known as saw-cut. Today, however, that method is almost obsolete because of its wastefulness, for as much wood is lost in saw dust as that actually used as veneer. They were much thicker than the knife-cut variety and had score marks left by the saw which had to be taken out on the side to be glued with the toothing plane (see page 20). Occasionally one may come across an odd parcel of saw-cut veneer and there is a limited production, but it is largely a thing of the past.

The methods of slicing veneers are shown diagrammatically in Fig. 1. That at A is flat slicing, the flitch being mounted on a heavy bed and a

Fig. 2 (below) Flat slicing machine showing flitch in position.

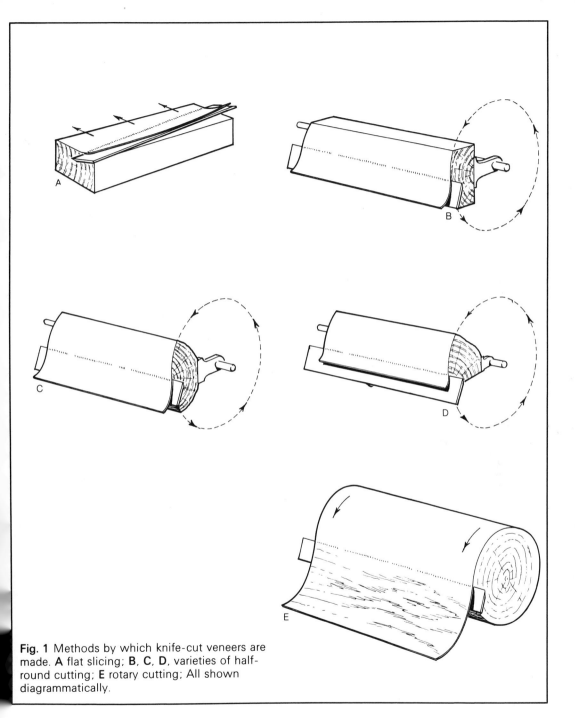

Fig. 1 Methods by which knife-cut veneers are made. **A** flat slicing; **B**, **C**, **D**, varieties of half-round cutting; **E** rotary cutting; All shown diagrammatically.

Fig. 3 (above) Veneer pack being trimmed on the guillotine.

knife passed across it. After each cut the flitch is raised by an amount equal to the required thickness of the veneer, and as the leaves are cut they are piled in the order of cutting. Generally, the knife is inclined at a slight angle. Fig. 2 shows a slicing machine. Some machines work vertically rather than horizontally.

Half-round or stay-log cutting is shown at Fig. 1B. The flitch is mounted off-centre and is revolved towards the knife. In this instance the flitch is mounted with its heart side towards the centre but owing to its being offset the knife does not follow the path of the annual rings but cuts at a slight angle across them. Timbers relying on the rays for their figure could not be cut by this method. At C, however, the flitch is mounted the other way round, and the first leaves would show ray figure, though this would decline with successive cuts. The arrangement at D is similar but the log has been quarter-cut first. All the methods may be used for decorative veneers. E is different,

however, and is known as rotary cutting, the log being mounted on a huge lathe-like machine and revolved towards a knife which moves in at a predetermined rate (decided by the required thickness of veneer). It thus peels the log in a continuous sheet. The resulting veneer, however, shows an uninteresting figure and has an unnatural look. It is generally used in the manufacture of plywood. An exception is in the production of bird's eye maple which relies for its effect on the small irregularities in the annual rings. It will be realized that in rotary cutting any defects such as knots become more prevalent in the resulting veneer as the centre of the log is approached.

Most logs are steamed before being cut to soften the fibres, and rotary cut veneers are trimmed to

Fig. 3A (above right) Cutting log into flitches on band re-saw.

Fig. 3B (below right) Flat slicing knife-cut veneer. The machine cuts eight to ten leaves per minute.

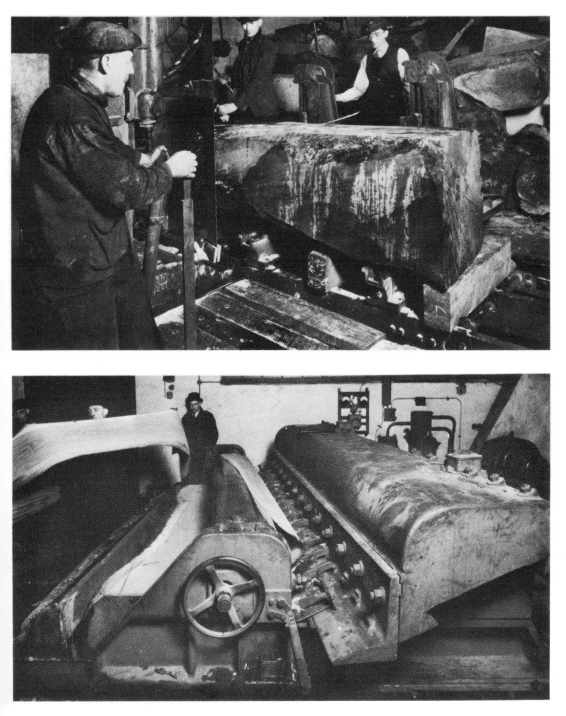

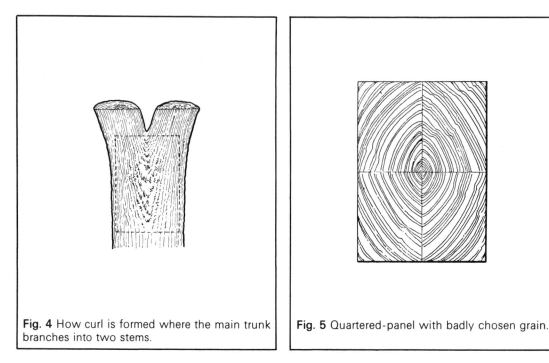

Fig. 4 How curl is formed where the main trunk branches into two stems.

Fig. 5 Quartered-panel with badly chosen grain.

the required size immediately after being cut, and are passed to a drying kiln which dries the veneer to the required moisture content. Flat sawn veneers are usually trimmed to size in packs on a huge guillotine (see Fig. 3).

There is a wide range of woods available as veneer. Apart from the usual cabinet woods there are varieties seldom or never seen in solid form. These include curls, burrs, butts, etc.

Curls. An example of the use of curls is given on page 81. The curl owes its figure to its position in the log at a point where the stem divides into two, or in the case of small curls to where a large branch springs out. The grain is of a wild character, and when cut takes the form roughly of a feather, the length of which is decided by the size of the two members or branch and the angle at which it leaves the trunk. It may vary from a few inches up to several feet in length. The grain is very short and diverse in direction, so that curls are brittle to handle. The merchant keeps them in piles as cut from the flitch so that when panels have to be matched they can be selected in pairs which have

practically identical figuring. Mahogany, satinwood, and walnut are typical woods producing curls. Butts are of a similar character, and are cut from the juncture of the larger roots. Walnut produces some extremely fine butts, and they are very effective when matched. Fig. 4 shows how the curl is formed where the trunk branches into two limbs.

Burrs. Burrs owe their existence to a growth on the outside of the trunk rather like a wart. They have a fine, small figuring which has something of the appearance of innumerable small knots closely packed together. The size is necessarily limited by that of the growth. One defect is that they are liable to pin-holes owing to the centres of the eyes and other small parts dropping out due to the short grain, and a liability to crumble under pressure from the knife. They often require to be patched as described on page 41. Walnut, elm, amboyna, sequoia, and ash yield burrs, though walnut is the most commonly used.

Another form of veneer is the oyster shell. It is not used much nowadays, though for reproductions of

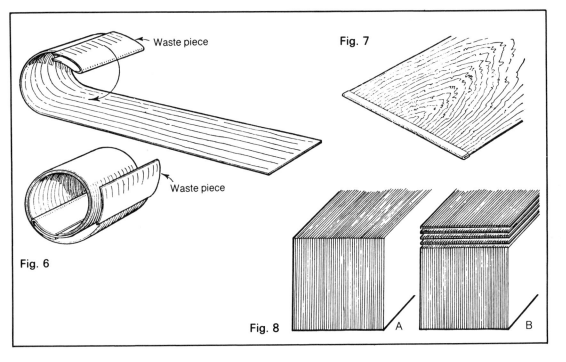

Waste piece

Fig. 7

Waste piece

Fig. 6

Fig. 8   A   B

Queen Anne furniture it is sometimes needed. It is cut from laburnum as a rule, the veneers being cut across the thickness of a branch, either square across or at an angle. They are naturally small, a few inches in diameter, and they are fitted side by side with straight joints between them.

Some timbers owe their figuring to the rays and they have, therefore, to be cut radially from the log. Figured oak is an example of this. Plain oak is also obtainable, in which case the cut is made across the rays rather than in line with them. Lacewood, which is the timber of the plane tree, is another example showing ray figuring. In most timbers, however, the rays play little part in the figuring, often being practically invisible. The beauty of many of the finer woods is due to the straight path of the knife or saw cutting across the undulations of the grain, the resulting effect being a series of streaks alternately light and dark running across the grain sometimes more or less at right angles or diagonally. In fiddleback mahogany the streaks are comparatively narrow and close together, whilst in rain mottle they are seen to be larger and more irregular.

Fig. 6 Rolling veneer to avoid splitting. Waste veneer is doubled around the end and the latter rolled inwards. Another waste piece is placed at the other end and the whole tied up.

Fig. 7 Taped end of veneer; advisable when veneer is stored to prevent splitting.

Fig. 8 Aroline and Fineline veneers. A packs of veneers glued together. B how pack is sliced.

Choice of veneers. When veneers are being selected for a piece of furniture, it should be remembered that the special figurings can be overdone. A cabinet might look delightful with, say, the doors covered with mahogany curls, but if the whole job had similar figuring it might become wearisome. It is a relief to have plain grain in part.

Another point to be considered is the direction of the grain. Curious optical illusions are sometimes unwittingly produced owing to the marked character of the grain taking the eye. Then, again, some treatments need a straight-grained timber, and unless a suitable kind is selected the result may be disappointing even though the figuring may be beautiful enough in itself. For instance, quartering needs a straight grain. The unfortunate effect of using a curved grain is shown in Fig. 5 in which the appearance is that of a badly shaped ellipse.

Handling veneer. All veneers are inclined to be brittle, though some varieties are worse than others. When being carried from the merchant they may have to be rolled, and to prevent splitting a piece of waste backing should be placed at the end. This supports the end and prevents a split from starting. Fig. 6 shows the idea. When being stored they should be kept humid to prevent cracking, and should lie flat between two boards. The best place is a ventilated cellar with artificial lighting.

Remember that the wild grain in some varieties, beautiful enough though it may be, makes the leaves liable to buckle. That they will buckle to an extent is unavoidable, and as explained in Chapter four they can be straightened out, but to allow a leaf to buckle is to make unnecessary work and in bad cases may result in cracking.

If veneers of wild grain are likely to be left lying about for a long time it is a wise precaution to glue tape at the ends as shown in Fig. 7 to prevent them from splitting. When required for use the tape is either cut right away or is removed by passing a swab damped in hot water along the tape.

When buying veneers examine the surface carefully. In a faulty leaf the surface may be torn out badly on one side, and even though it is laid with the defects inwards, it will probably show later owing to the glue shrinking and pulling in the veneer. This tearing out will often occur in just one half of a badly cut leaf, and is generally due to the knife being taken right across the log. At the beginning of the cut the veneer does not tear, but after the centre has been passed the fibres lift badly. In the best veneer the log is cut into flitches so that the cut is towards the centre only.

It is sometimes recommended that veneers are laid in the same position as cut from the flitch, that is, the exposed surface on the job should be that

Fig. 9 (below) Examples of Aroline veneers.

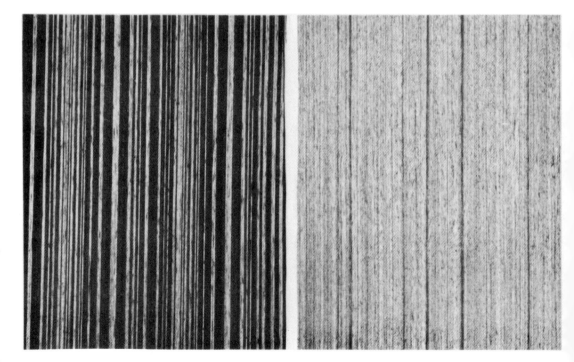

exposed in the flitch. Actually there is not a great deal in this if veneer is well cut, and in the case of a matched panel one leaf has obviously to be laid the reverse way. If a matched panel is examined, no difference will be seen—unless, of course, badly cut veneer with torn-out grain has been used.

Hard, heavy veneers, such as ebony and rosewood, should not be laid on a softwood, as the latter will absorb most of the glue even when sized. Choose a harder wood such as mahogany or else cross-veneer first.

In the trade a great deal of veneer known as *Aroline* or *Fineline* veneer is used for commercial furniture, fitments, etc. It is not, however, generally available to the man in the street. In manufacture veneers are glued together in packs of several hundred veneers (Fig. 8A), and when set are sliced into veneers in a right angles direction as at B so that the resulting veneer shows the edges of the leaves, the effect being that of natural wood with perfectly straight grain. Some of the veneers are darker than others and are arranged in the packs so that a striped effect is obtained. The great advantage of the veneer is that fifty or so identical items can be made all with practically the same grain effect, whereas with natural grain veneers no two items could have the same figuring. Fig. 9 shows two pieces of *Aroline* veneers.

Veneer timbers. The following list gives the veneers chiefly used in furniture making, and their characteristics, but it should be realized that the supply of many of them is uncertain, and some may be entirely unobtainable. As regards their cost it is clearly impossible to give any indication at all, as prices are liable to fluctuate not only with supply, but also according to the financial position generally. It can only be said that the price may vary widely in accordance with the quality of the figure, soundness, and size.

It is always advisable to obtain all the veneer required for a single job at the same time, because some logs have individual colour or figure peculiar to themselves. It may be impossible to obtain a similar veneer later. This may not apply to the plainer types of veneer, but it is certainly true of many of the choice fancy woods. The man who buys only a small quantity of veneer in lesser sizes can often get what he wants by buying small parcels of mixed veneers. Many merchants make a practice of supplying these, and they are cheaper because they contain odd ends which are quite sound, but for which the merchant would have no sale to the trade.

Amboyna. A richly mottled veneer of yellowish-gold shade. Mostly small and irregular in shape.
Ash Burr. A creamy-coloured wood, liable to small black bark ingrowths.
Ash, English. A light wood, sometimes with fiddle mottle figure. Obtainable only in narrow widths, as edge is very sappy and nearly all ash has a brown heart.
Ash, Tamo (Japanese). A rare ash, light in colour and with rather large figuring.
Avodire. A beautiful light yellow wood with mottle striped figure.
Black Bean (Australian). Medium brown in colour. Expensive as it is difficult to cut, since it tends to become brittle, and may cause the polish to crack.
Birch, Canadian White. A wood with large figure available in two colours, white or dark (the white being the sap wood and the dark the heart wood). The dark is known as betula.
Birch, Masur. A light wood with small figure having dark streaks.
Bubinga. A warm brown veneer with striped straight grain.
Courbaril. This wood varies in figure. It is striped with light and dark brown.
Ebony, Macassar. Deep brown in colour with almost black streaks. This wood is prone to contain small hair shakes or cracks—hence the narrow widths.
Elm. Light tan colour sometimes with fine swirling figure.
Elm Burr. Varies from reddish-brown to cream.
Greywood, Indian Silver. Somewhat similar in colour to walnut. When quartered the veneer has a straight, striped effect, but when cut across the tree the figure and colour are more varied.
Laurel, Indian. A fine medium-brown wood with light and dark streaks. Every log varies much in colour, figure and grain.
Mahogany. There are innumerable varieties of this, the two main groups being the Swietenia, which includes Cuban, St. Domingo, Belize, Honduras, Tobasco; and the Knaya group, which comes from Africa. The American mahoganies are not so hard as those from the West Indies, and that

producing the finest figure is the Cuban, though it is now scarce. All the Swietenia group, however, produce fine veneers. The African varieties are softer in texture and fade more quickly.

Of the curls the Cuban is the most reliable, followed by the Honduras variety; the African curl is liable to develop cracks after polishing. Other figures include the straight stripe of the Sapele; the irregular stripe broken by a mottle; the rich roe of the Honduras often again broken by a cross figure; the bee's wing of the Cuban variety; the dapple figure; the fiddle back, and so on.

Maple, Bird's Eye. Being rotary cut, this is obtainable in great widths.

Burr, Maple. A beautiful burr, but irregular in shape, liable to bark ingrowths. Varies in colour from a light beige shade to a pinkish coloration.

Maple, Quilted. A light wood with a large figure. A stout gauge should be used, as this wood is liable to glue penetration.

Oak. There are many varieties of this, of which the English is the finest, producing an extremely fine figure with silver grain. Austrian and Russian oaks also produce fine woods and are milder. Japanese oak is a dense wood of slight, delicate figure. English brown oak and pollard oak are especially fine, being of a rich deep brown shade beautifully marked.

Oak, Figured British. The classification of figure in oak may be roughly divided into small, medium, and heavy figure.

Oak, English Brown. A rich brown shade caused by a fungus which produces discoloration.

Obeche. A light yellow softwood.

Padouk, Indian. A reddish-brown wood with narrow striped figure.

Peroba. Richly figured, yellowish in colour.

Rosewood, Bombay. Deep brown in colour tending to purple.

Rosewood, Rio. Lighter in colour than the above.

Satinwood, East Indian. Finely figured golden yellow wood.

Sycamore, English. A fine hard white wood liable to tone down in time. Grey sycamore (harewood) is immersed in a solution which, by chemical action with the acid in the wood, turns it to a fine silver grey. Weathered sycamore is of a very light brown shade.

Teak. A hard wood of a sombre brown shade.

Thuya. This produces fine burrs somewhat like Amboyna, but lacks the golden colour of the latter.

Walnut. There are many varieties of this, of which the most usual are the French, Italian, American, Circassian, Australian, and English (though the latter is rare nowadays). The Italian is generally darker than the French. American walnut is straighter in the grain and of a purple-brown shade. The varieties of figuring can be roughly classified as follows:

Walnut, Plain. Obtainable with straight grain suitable for quartering, and with more curly but plain figuring.

Walnut, Butt. With fine feather-like grain. In some cases a leaf is plain for the greater part and has butt figuring at one end.

Walnut, Burr. A choice veneer having small mottled grain.

Zebrano. A strongly marked wood with dark brown stripes on a light background. The veneer is somewhat inclined to buckle.

Dyed veneers. These are available in many shades, but should be used with care as the effect can look unnatural and appear startling.

Chapter four

Preparation of veneer

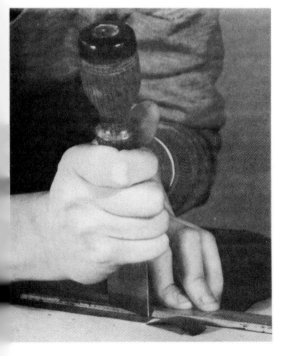

Knife-cut veneers are cut with the chisel or knife. The veneer is supported on a flat board and is held down with the straight-edge. Fig. 1 shows the cutting operation. Generally it is advisable to cut across the grain first, so that if the edge should split away under the pressure, the following cut *with* the grain will remove the split portion. Care is needed when cutting *with* the grain to avoid the chisel following the grain and so drifting from the straight-edge.

In large shops special trimming machines are often installed, these working on the guillotine principle.

Use of cutting gauge. For cross-banding work several narrow strips are often needed, and these are best cut with the cutting gauge as in Fig. 2. The veneer is laid across a board with the edge overhanging slightly, and a batten is placed across it just sufficiently far from the edge to clear the end of the gauge. Its purpose is to prevent the veneer from buckling. It is pressed tightly down and the fence of the gauge kept lightly against the edge of the veneer. Knife-cut veneers can generally be cut right through in this way, but thicker veneers need to be reversed and a second cut made on the opposite side.

When the bandings are to be laid on a surface to overhang at both sides the strips can be gauged straight off one after the other. If, however, they have to form a joint, as in the case of a banding laid around a panel, it is necessary to trim the edge with the plane before each cut is made. The trimmed edge should be marked so that it can be easily identified.

Trimming the edges. Fig. 3 shows how veneer is trimmed. It is placed on the shooting-board with the edge overhanging slightly, and a batten pressed tightly down over it. A metal panel or jointing plane is the best tool to use for the purpose. When a number of pieces have to be trimmed for jointing they can be fixed between two battens with thumbscrews, as in Fig. 4, and all be planed at the same time.

Some veneers with tricky grain are very liable to flake away when being planed, and the best way of

Fig. 1 (left) Cutting veneer with chisel and straight-edge.

dealing with these is to fix a thin batten at each side with thumbscrews right at the edge. The plane removes shavings from the battens as well as the veneer. The close support at both sides prevents the tendency to chip out. Alternatively gummed tape can be stuck to the veneer.

Continuity of grain. It sometimes happens that the front of a piece of furniture has to be laid with a single sheet of veneer such as a curl, and it is most important that the separate pieces are given an identification number so that they can be laid on the drawer fronts and rails in the correct order. Fig. 5 is a chest of this kind. A centre line is drawn down the veneer and the widths of the fronts and rails marked upon it with a trifle added to allow for cleaning off. The allowance should be reduced to a minimum so as not to interfere with the continuity of the grain. The lines are drawn as Fig. 6 and the

Fig. 2 (left) Cutting cross-banding with cutting gauge.

Fig. 3 (below) Trimming veneer for cross-banding on the shooting board.

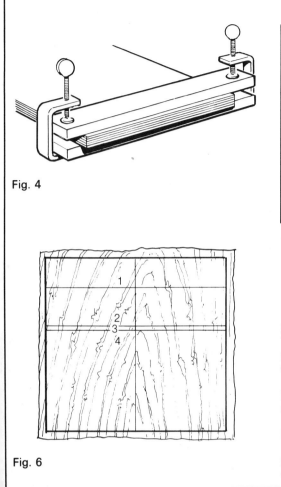

Fig. 4

Fig. 5

Fig. 6

Fig. 4 Trimming several thicknesses of veneer. Two battens are thumbscrewed across to prevent buckling. The edges are planed on the shooting-board.

Fig. 5 Item with doors and drawers showing continuous grain.

Fig. 6 Veneer marked to show continuous grain. In a simple case like this numbering is scarcely necessary, but for an item with many parts it would be essential.

parts numbered consecutively. When laid, the centre lines are made to coincide with centre lines drawn on the drawer fronts and their rails.

Quartered panels. When cutting out veneers for a quartered panel it is an advantage to use four consecutive sheets of veneer because then any peculiarities in the grain will be balanced in the four pieces as shown at Fig. 7A. Two of the pieces, of course, will be reversed when being assembled. One objection to this is that it can be rather wasteful, since it means cutting into four sheets,

and for this reason it is sometimes avoided, the four pieces being marked out from a single sheet. When this is done it is important that the grain is as straight as possible so that its slope in the rectangles marked out is the same in all cases. The unfortunate effect of not noting this is shown at Fig. 7C, in which the grain curves away at one end. The consequence is that in the end piece the grain runs through it almost in line with the sides, with the result that the completed panel looks like that at B. Quartered panels are dealt with more fully, however, in Chapter nine, Built-up panels 1.

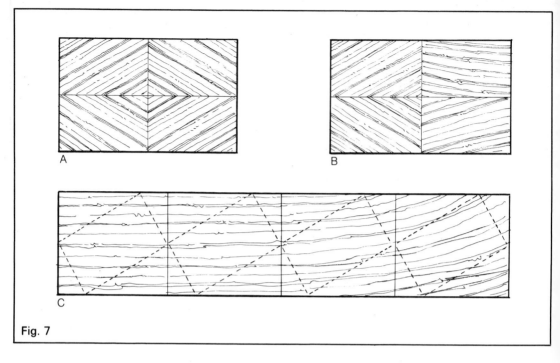

A

B

C

Fig. 7

Fig. 7 Points to note when making a quartered panel. At **A** the four pieces are properly balanced. The unfortunate effect at **B** is the result of marking out the pieces from a strip in which the grain curves away as as **C**. In the best work the pieces are cut from four consecutive leaves of veneer so that the grain is balanced exactly.

Saw-cut veneer. This is seldom seen today, but odd packets of it do occasionally come to light. To cut it it is necessary to use a fine-toothed saw as in Fig. 8. The veneer is held down on a flat board and a straight-edge cramped down over the two. The saw is moved along this. Originally the cabinet maker kept a special saw for the purpose. It had a curved edge as shown in Fig. 9, and there was thus no liability for the ends of the saw to dig in. For small pieces of veneer pressure from the hand over the straight-edge is sufficient, but for a wide leaf the cramps are essential.

If saw-cut veneer is closely examined it will be seen that both sides have prominent marks made by the circular saw in manufacture, and it is essential that these are removed on the lower side (that which faces the groundwork) before it is laid. Many an otherwise fine piece of cabinet work has been spoilt by neglecting this simple precaution. The mischief of it is that when first laid and cleaned up the result seems quite satisfactory. The trouble comes several months later when the glue has shrunk to the full. This is due to the roughness of the underside of the veneer caused by the circular saw. It takes the form of innumerable fine ridges and depressions of a semi-circular shape, the curve being that of the saw by which they were cut. In the depressions a thickness of glue is imprisoned and in course of time this shrinks and pulls down the surface slightly, as in Fig. 10. Thus a series of fine curves can be detected right across the surface, and these look particularly bad if the job is french polished, because they catch and reflect the light.

Such an effect is often put down to bad cleaning-up, but the probability is that the surface was perfect when first polished and has developed the blemish since, simply because the ridges on the underside were not rubbed down.

36

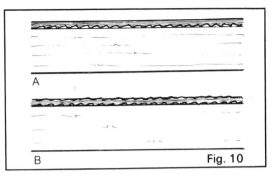

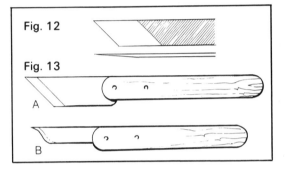

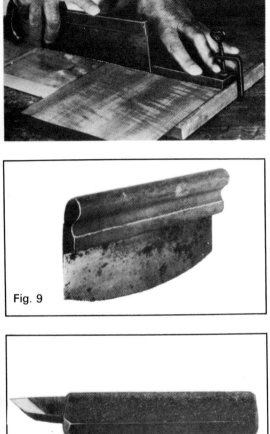

Fig. 9

Fig. 11

Fig. 8 (top left) Cutting veneer with saw held against a straight-edge.

Fig. 9 (centre left) Veneer saw.

Fig. 10 Saw marks in veneer. Glue in indentations at underside shrinks and pulls down surface as at **B**. Hence necessity for toothing before laying.

Fig. 11 (bottom left) Knife for patching veneer. Blade made from old file or hack-saw blade.

Fig. 12 Side and top view of veneer patching knife made from an old hack-saw blade or thin file.

Fig. 13 Useful veneering knives.

The toothing plane is used to remove the saw marks. It should be sharpened carefully and set fine to avoid tearing, and be worked in all directions until all saw marks are taken out. The veneer must be laid on a flat board so that it has close support, and this should be examined to see that there are no chips beneath the veneer, as these would cause the latter to stand up locally and the toothing would make it thin. Special care must be taken when working the plane at the edges to avoid cracking the veneer so causing damage which cannot be repaired.

Blemishes in veneer. Certain veneers are liable to show holes or cracks, and these have to be made good before laying. In many cases this is done by the veneer manufacturer, otherwise it is necessary to place a piece of veneer of similar grain beneath the blemish, and cut through both

37

with a keen knife having a thin point, such as that shown in Figs. 11 and 12. There is something rather special about this knife. It must be thin and the sharpened bevel at as low an angle as possible because it is important that the cut in the veneer is really narrow. Usually it is made by the worker himself from an old hacksaw blade and sometimes from a thin file. A second bevel such as that sharpened on a chisel would be useless as the wedge form would make too thick a cut. Instead there is just a flat bevel as in Fig. 12. Other knives sometimes used are shown in Fig. 13.

To enable a close match to be made a 'window' slightly larger than the defect is cut in the veneer as in Fig. 14. This enables the grain of the patch to be matched closely when placed beneath. Those doing the work for the first time may prefer to hold the patch in position with strips of gummed tape stuck on the underside. The shape of the patch is cut through both thicknesses and is obviously larger than the 'window' as shown in Fig. 15. The knife is held at a *slight* angle so that it undercuts the veneer. In this way the patch is the merest trifle larger than that in the main veneer and

so makes a close fit. Generally it has to be inserted from beneath owing to the slight angle of the edges.

Considerable pressure is needed for the cut which is made freehand. The shape depends upon the form of the blemish. Sometimes the simple shape shown in Fig. 16B is suitable. In others the saw tooth shape in Fig. 15 is better. The important point is to keep the cuts as far as possible in line with the grain. Thus in Fig. 17 only the ends of the cuts slope across the grain and then only at a slight angle. In Fig. 15 the saw tooth cuts are at a flat angle so that the 'teeth' are long and narrow. In this way the patch scarcely shows. In other cases the grain of the veneer can be followed almost entirely as in Fig. 19. The blemish is shown at A, and B, which is an adjoining leaf of veneer, shows the cut and beneath it the patch.

When a second cut is needed care must be taken to follow the path of the first cut exactly. It depends

Fig. 15 (below) Cutting patch in veneer. Window enables grain to be matched.

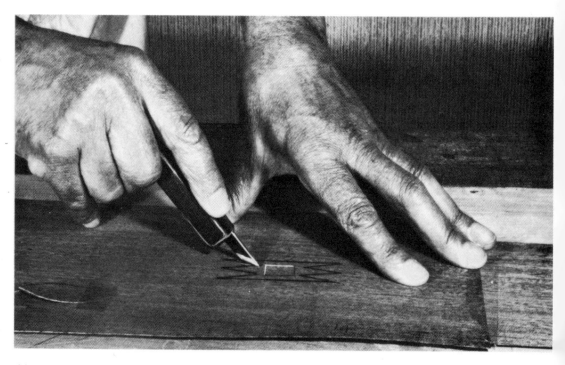

upon the particular wood of the veneer and its thickness. Some tough woods take a lot of cutting through, and sometimes as many as three cuts may be needed. However, a single cut through both thicknesses is more satisfactory. In many woods such as walnut, sapele, mahogany, etc., it is easily achieved, but with some woods a second cut is unavoidable. Remember to hold the knife at a slight angle. If the angle is too pronounced the patch will be too large, whereas there will be a loose fit if the knife is held vertical. One important point is that the veneer must be held down on a flat board. Any indentations or obstructions may cause the knife to break through and cause damage.

Having completed the cut the patch piece is removed and the patch itself placed in the hole in the main veneer. It often has to go in from beneath. It is rubbed down with the cross-peen of

Fig. 17 (below) Simple shape suitable for small defect. Patch shown to the left.

Fig. 18 (bottom) Patch in which shape follows the line of the grain.

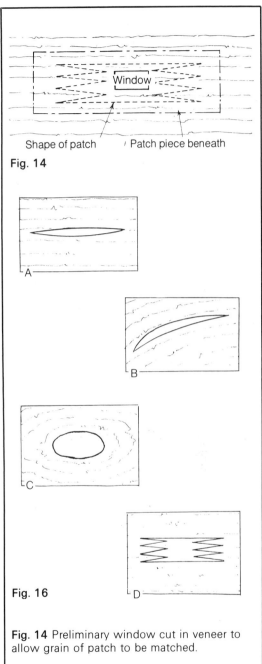

Fig. 14

Shape of patch   Patch piece beneath

Fig. 16

Fig. 14 Preliminary window cut in veneer to allow grain of patch to be matched.

Fig. 16 Shape of patches.

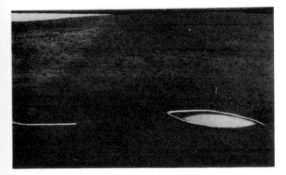

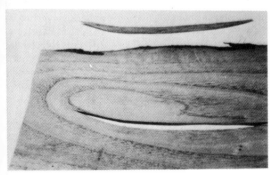

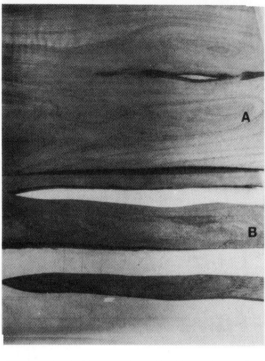

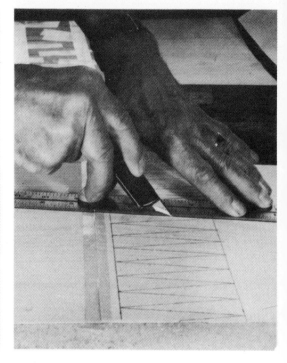

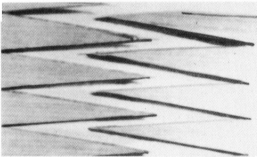

Fig. 19 (above left) Patching veneer. **A** obvious blemish at end of veneer leaf. **B** adjoining leaf having same blemish cut away. The patch is shown below.

Fig. 20 (below left) Length finger joint. The parts are shown separated.

Fig. 21 (above right) Cutting the length finger joint using a straight-edge. The experienced man usually cuts the shape freehand.

the hammer or with the wooden handle of the knife if the end is flat and straight.

When a long strip of veneer has to be lengthened an almost invisible joint can be made by making V cuts as in Fig. 20. The two pieces are placed together with an overlap long enough to include the V shapes with a little spare at each end. The grain of course should be matched closely. The pieces are held together with gummed tape to prevent movement and long sloping cuts made as in Fig. 21. Again, the knife is held at a slight angle so that it

undercuts the veneer, the slope being reversed at each side of the V. The usual plan is to mark on the veneer the extent of the V cuts with pencil or chalk, and the tradesman usually marks the cuts freehand by judgement. There is no need to mark the width of the V's because, when carefully done, the joint cannot be seen. The small patch in Fig. 15 follows the same V cut idea, and is particularly successful because none of the cuts is directly across the grain. A light wood such as sycamore or ash needs a light glue; flake white powder has sometimes to be added to avoid a dark appearance.

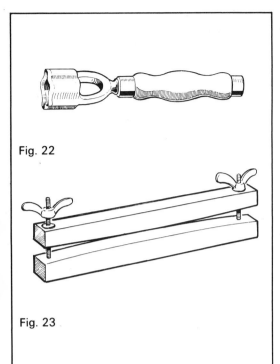

Fig. 22

Fig. 23

Fig. 22 Interwood patented punch for repairing veneers. In later pattern punches an ejector enables the cut-out veneer to be removed from the punch easily.

Fig. 23 Useful cramps for flatting veneers. They are slightly bowed at the centre so that pressure is applied in the middle first. The veneer is placed between cauls.

In all work of this kind, whether patching or lengthening, the grain must be matched closely. This necessitates the patch having similar grain to that of the main veneer. There is more in it than this, however, particularly for woods such as sapele. If the latter is viewed from one direction it will show light and dark streaks. When seen from the other direction the parts that were light now appear dark and vice versa. This is due to the grain in one streak being inclined at an angle in the opposite direction from that of those adjoining. Consequently the streaks of the patch piece must have the same grain characteristics. Otherwise the patch will be only too glaringly obvious. Generally an offcut of the same leaf or one adjoining is used for the patch, and if the surface of both this and the veneer are lightly dampened the light and dark streaks will be obvious.

Some large shops use a special jigsaw fitted with a fine blade like a fretsaw to cut the veneer. The table is tilted a trifle so that the thickness of the saw-cut is taken up when the parts are interchanged. Veneers in woods such as burr walnut frequently have holes and cracks, and the veneer manufacturer usually has a series of special punches made in various sizes and shapes. This cuts a piece bodily out of the veneer, and another piece of veneer cut with the same punch is inserted. A punch is shown in Fig. 22.

One last point is that it is an advantage to lay strips of gummed tape across curls in a sloping direction before laying. This helps to prevent cracking.

Flatting veneers. In all these processes it is assumed that the veneer is flat, but complications sometimes arise owing to the veneer being buckled. The trouble is not limited to the fact that it may be awkward to place a batten flat across it. The real problem is that the buckling prevents the edge from being straight, because when released from the pressure of the batten it springs back to another shape. This necessitates flatting the veneer.

One way of doing this is to damp the veneer on both sides with a swab—not to make it soaking wet, but damp enough to render it pliable. Two flat cauls of wood slightly larger than the veneer are then heated thoroughly and are cramped one each side of the veneer. After an hour or so when the moisture has evaporated the veneer should be flat. Sometimes a second cauling is necessary. Apart from its flatting effect, this process is useful on such woods as rosewood, satinwood, and teak, as it helps to draw out the oil which prevents the glue from holding well. In these cases, unless the veneer is buckled, there is no need to damp the veneer. Fig. 23 shows a form of cramp often used in flatting.

After the operation the veneer should be jointed and laid as soon as possible, because there is always a tendency for it to become buckled again.

Fig 24 Trimming a veneer pack along the length in the guillotine. Photograph by courtesy of Aaronson Brothers Ltd.

It will be realized that the cauls must either be of a single width of wood or else battens must be fixed across the outside. If a jointed caul is used the heat will probably cause the joint to give unless assembled with resin glue.

Another method of flatting, and one which the writer prefers, is to damp the veneer slightly with very thin glue size and place it between two flat pieces of wood with a medium weight above. I left overnight the veneer will be flat and dry by th morning ready for use. A large number of veneer can be stacked in this way, a board being place above each leaf. The advantage is that the metho is less violent and is not liable to cause crack through rapid shrinking with the heat. If necessar the heat method could be used afterwards.

This flatting process is a good idea for any built-u designs in veneer which are to be laid with th caul, because it shrinks the veneer and goes a lon way towards preventing joints from opening.

Chapter five

Veneer presses, etc.

In the trade presses are used to the almost entire exclusion of hand methods, though the types of presses used vary with the requirements of the particular trade. The manufacturer who makes only veneer panels to standard sizes uses the multi-plate thermostatically-controlled press or the short-cycle continuous press. Taking first the former, the time during which the press is occupied by one batch of panels is cut to the minimum since resin glue is used which is heat cured. The platens may be electrically heated or heated with hot water, and the pressing time (varying with the type of glue and the temperature) may be a few minutes only, leaving the press free for another batch of panels. An example of the type is given in Fig. 1. Other models take up to eight panels at one pressing. The hydraulic press in Fig. 2 has a single opening but three tables which can be operated singly, in pairs, or three as a single unit.

Fig. 1 The electric multi-platen hydraulic press type HEP from Interwood Limited features an interlocked frame and fully laid out, electrically heated, thermostatically controlled platens.

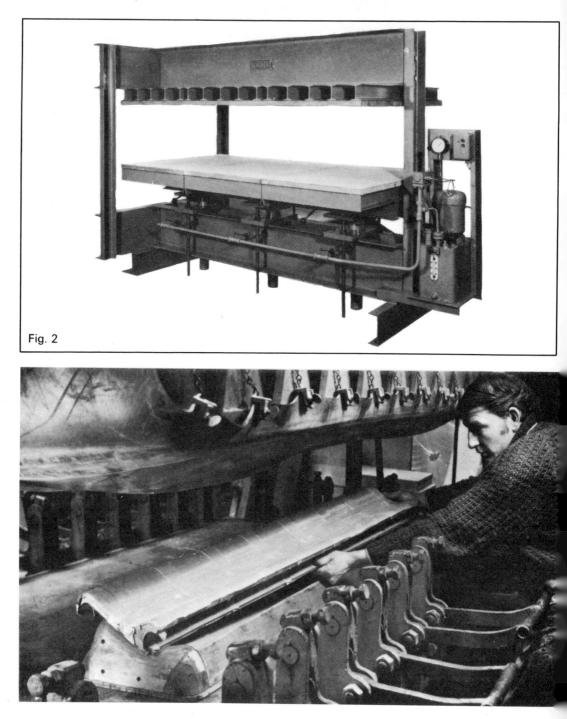

Fig. 2

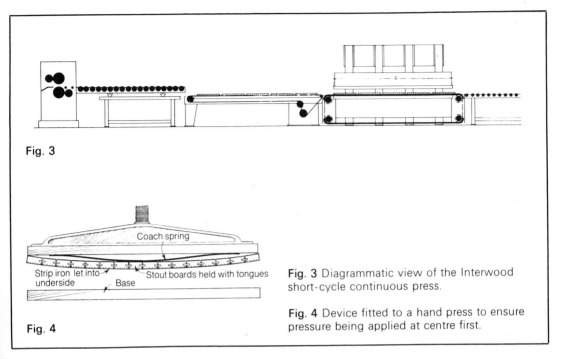

Fig. 3

Coach spring

Strip iron let into
underside
Base
Stout boards held with tongues

Fig. 4

Fig. 3 Diagrammatic view of the Interwood short-cycle continuous press.

Fig. 4 Device fitted to a hand press to ensure pressure being applied at centre first.

The short-cycle continuous press is shown diagrammatically in Fig. 3. In this the panels pass through a glue spreader at one end, and are conveyed on rollers to a table on which the veneers are added. From here they pass to a thermostatically-controlled press in which the pressing time can be as low as less than one minute depending upon the glue/hardener mixture. On completion the panels are ejected, again passing on rollers to a loading trolley. Small panels can be veneered side by side as well as large individual panels.

In workshops where occasional veneering has to be done, as distinct from factories where veneering is the sole process, manually operated presses are still used. They vary, some are for single panels, others have three adjacent platens which can be operated singly or as a whole for large panels.

Fig. 2 (above left) Schubert hydraulic cold press, model Universal fitted with Open End.

Fig. 2A (below left) Veneer of a piano fall being pressed in a compressed air press.

Sometimes trouble is experienced in this form of press owing to splits and bubbles appearing in the centre of the panel. It is invariably due to the glue being unable to escape at the edges and is caused by the flat shape of the cauls. It has already been stressed elsewhere that the pressure should be applied at the centre first, and it is obvious that with a single-screw press this cannot be done if the caul is flat. An excellent way of overcoming the difficulty is shown in Fig. 4 in which the main upper bed is made of a series of strips about 75mm. (3in.) by 50mm. (2in.) in section fitted loosely together with tongues, but prevented from separating by three or four bands of strip iron let into and screwed to the lower surface. The whole thing is secured at each side to the metal cross-beams. Between the last-named and bearing on the upper side of the strips are fixed two or three coach springs. Thus the normal shape of the bed is a bow, and when the screw is tightened the pressure is necessarily felt in the centre first. As it is screwed right up the springs flatten out and the whole thing is pressed out all over.

It is a golden rule in work of this kind always to see

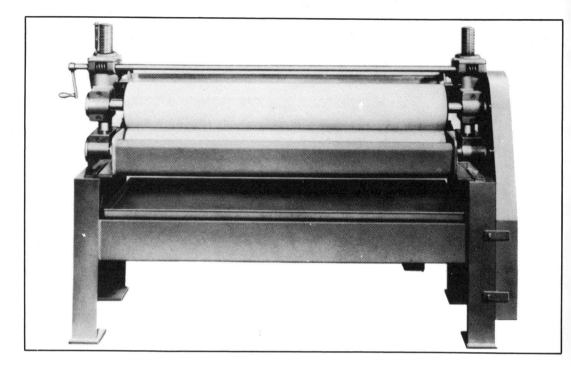

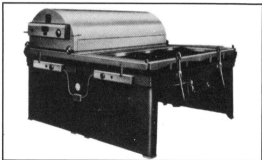

Fig. 5 (above) Glue spreading machine. Photograph by courtesy of Interwood Limited.

Fig. 6 (left) Continuous production twin shaping veneering press. Photograph by courtesy of Interwood Limited.

Fig. 7 Diagram showing the working of the Harefield envelope.

Fig. 8 Sectional view of envelope in use.

that the glue is pressed out before the pressure is applied at the edges. This is specially the case when the glue is applied by hand. When an automatic spreader is available it does not matter so much, because the amount to be pressed out is far less than when it is brushed on. The great virtue of the spreader is that it applies just the right amount equally all over, and the waste is incomparably less. This is especially essential today in view of the high cost of resin glue. Fig 5 is an example of a spreader.

In another class is the vacuum press used for

shaped work. This is fitted with a rubber sheet which is passed over the work piece, and the air beneath pumped out. The pliable rubber presses closely down over the work by atmospheric pressure so that the veneer conforms closely to the shaped groundwork. The Interwood twin-table press is shown in Fig. 6. In this the tailored veneer is placed over the groundwork, the frame with rubber sheet lowered over it and the air beneath pumped out. The electrically-heated dome is drawn forward over it and left until curing time has been completed. In the meantime the second table

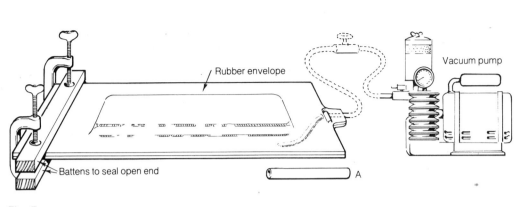

Rubber envelope

Vacuum pump

Battens to seal open end

A

Fig. 7

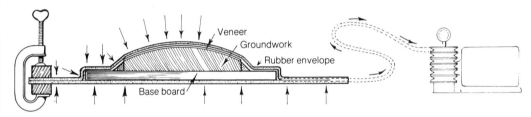

Veneer
Groundwork
Rubber envelope

Base board

Fig. 8

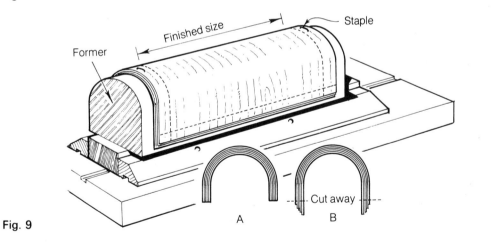

Finished size

Staple

Former

Cut away

A

B

Fig. 9

Fig. 9 Set-up for a laminated semi-circular member.

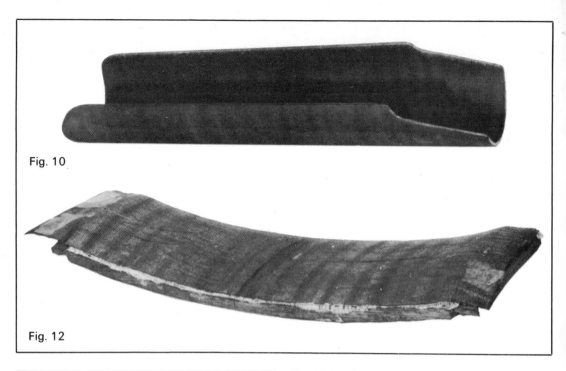

Fig. 10

Fig. 12

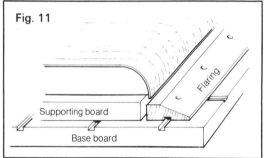

Fig. 11

Fig. 10 Laminated semi-circular work piece, shape completed.

Fig. 11 Panel with coved edges.

Fig. 12 Work piece of compound curvature.

work which is shaped on both sides (see Fig. 12). Fig. 9 shows how a laminated semi-circular item is made. An internal former is needed and is mounted upon a waste strip to enable the envelope to wrap closely to the veneer edges, and grooved flaring pieces are placed at each side. In such an acute curve it is advisable to cover the top veneer with gummed tape to prevent cracking. The laminae are glued and held to the former with staples at each end and the whole covered with newspaper. The set-up is placed in the envelope and battens cramped to the open end to seal it (see Fig. 7). The vacuum pump is started and left in operation until curing time has been completed (depending upon the adhesive used and the temperature). Fig. 10 shows the completed shape.

with its rubber sheet has been loaded and the full vacuum created. As soon as the glue line of the first table has been cured (notified by an alarm clock) the dome may be drawn forward over the second table for curing.

Similar in principle is the Harefield Supasheet envelope used in conjunction with a vacuum pump. Fig. 7 and 8 show diagrammatically the principle of operation from which it will be seen that a flat baseboard is used to prevent distortion, though for some work this may not be needed, particularly

Fig. 13 (top) View of the rubber Harefield envelope with complicated work pieces of compound shaping.

Fig. 14 (centre) Veneer trimming machine. Photograph by courtesy of Interwood Limited.

In the case of a panel with coved edges the veneer is cut with extra length so that it projects beyond the curve. A supporting board slightly smaller than the work is placed beneath, and both are placed on a baseboard having criss-cross grooves to enable air to be withdrawn evenly. A flaring is added at the coved edges as shown in Fig. 11. It will be realized that flat panels can be veneered in this way, but of course it is in shaped work that the full advantage is felt. A compound shape is shown in Fig. 12. Fig. 13 shows the envelope used for pressing more complicated shapes.

In the trade many other machines are used for various purposes such as jointing, trimming, (Fig. 14), splicing, veneer banding and lipping, but these are found only in the larger workshops in which veneering only is done.

Circular table veneered with Rio rosewood. This series of photographs shows the various stages of the veneering process. The groundwork is of lamin board, and on this was first laid a counter veneer, this being quartered so that the radiating grain of the face veneers was at right angles with it.

Fig. 15 (opposite above) Glue is being applied with a glue spreader.

Fig. 16 (opposite below) The radiating face veneers are pulled back to show the counter-veneers beneath.

Fig. 17 (above) The face veneers are taped together ready to be passed into the press.

Fig. 18 (right) The finished table.

The table was made by D. Bianco & Sons Ltd. to whom we are indebted for this information. Photographs by courtesy of Ciba-Geigy (U.K.) Ltd.

Chapter six

Caul veneering

This is the method used by men who have no press facilities, and for work for which the use of the veneering hammer would be impracticable. In common with press veneering, it can be used for most veneering operations, and is essential for difficult woods, built-up patterns, and for marquetry. The requirements are simple but a large number of cramps is needed—at any rate for work of any great size. The caul itself is a panel of wood planed perfectly flat and if possible without joints. If the latter are unavoidable there must be cross-battens screwed on at the back when Scotch glue is used otherwise the joints may fail owing to the heat used in the process. If, however, the joints are put together with resin glue there is no need for the battens because resin does not soften under heat. Sometimes a sheet of zinc is used, this being backed by a wood panel. One advantage of the zinc is that it retains its heat longer than wood.

The purpose of the caul is to press the veneer into close contact with the groundwork and to press out surplus glue. In the case of fairly wide work there is the danger that when the cramps are applied at the edges (as they have to be) the centre part may not be under pressure, and the surplus glue, instead of being expelled at the edges, may be driven towards the centre where it is trapped. To avoid this the cramps are applied over pairs of cross-bearers which have slightly curved edges as in Fig. 1. Thus when the cramps are tightened the pressure is felt at the middle first, so driving surplus glue outwards. For the same reason the middle cross-bearers are applied before the end ones.

Shape of the bearers. The bearers can be of 25mm. (1in.) stuff or more in thickness by about 50mm. (2in.) wide, though these measurements may vary in accordance with the size of the work being done. They are placed on edge across the caul, and their purpose is to provide pressure right across the work. The curved edges are placed inwards so that when the cramps are applied at the ends the centre receives the pressure

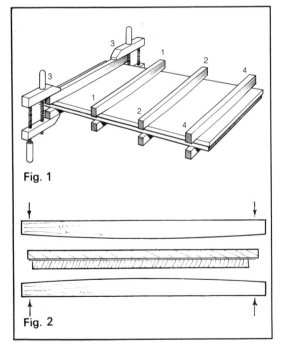

Fig. 1

Fig. 2

Fig. 1 Order in which cramps are tightened over cross-bearers in caul veneering.

Fig. 2 Shape of cross-bearers. The curve is slightly exaggerated.

first. The cramps can be of the ordinary G type, or the handscrew variety. To avoid distortion, the bearers are in pairs and all have the same degree of curvature, so that the forces cancel each other out and the work remains flat (see Fig. 2).

A practical example

Assume that a panel about 76·2cm. (30in.) by 50·8cm. (20in.) is to be veneered on one side only. The groundwork is prepared in the way

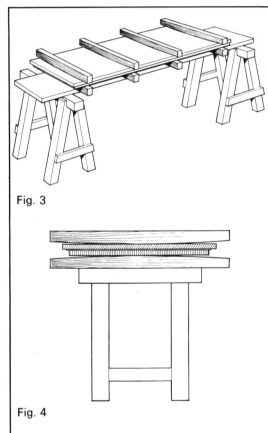

Fig. 3

Fig. 4

Fig. 3 Work laid out ready for caul. Everything should be prepared in advance as far as possible so that the cramps can be applied without loss of time.

Fig. 4 Work on bench for cramping.

already described. Its surface is toothed, and if of softwood it is sized. A caul slightly larger than the groundwork is needed, enough sheets of newspaper to cover the whole, four pairs of bearers, and eight handscrews or G cramps. The veneer is cut out to size to overhang about 10mm. (⅜in.) all round (this is assuming that the entire surface has to be covered: if it is to be cross-banded it should stand in a trifle), and both it and the groundwork are wiped free of dust.

If Scotch glue is being used a coat is brushed over both the groundwork and the veneer. There is no hurry about this, because it does not matter if the glue does chill. In fact, there is an advantage in allowing it to do so. When the caul is applied later there is a tendency for the veneer to float. This does not matter a great deal in a plain sheet of veneer providing there is still an overhang all round, but in the case of a matched or built-up pattern it is important that it remains exactly in position. Allowing the glue to chill helps a great deal in this respect, though in matched panels the additional precaution of driving in fine veneer pins is taken. This is dealt with more fully in Chapter nine. When the veneer is in position a sheet of newspaper is laid on top to prevent the caul from adhering.

A second advantage of allowing the glue to dry out is that the veneer shrinks after swelling with the liquid glue. Then, if the caul is pressed down rapidly the veneer is prevented from swelling as the heat liquefies the glue, since the pressure grips the veneer in position. This means less liability for the veneer to shrink later as the moist glue dries out, and consequent reduced tendency to pull hollow.

Applying the caul. It is now ready for the application of the caul, and it is here that one has to be fairly speedy when Scotch glue is used. Everything should be placed ready for use so that no time is lost. Handscrews should be opened the right amount, and, if an assistant is helping, the work each is to do should be decided. In this connection it should be noted that a helper is essential in a big job, so that the pairs of hand-screws can be tightened up simultaneously. Fig. 3 shows how the work is laid on bearers beneath. A bench could be used just as well providing the cross-bearers could project from

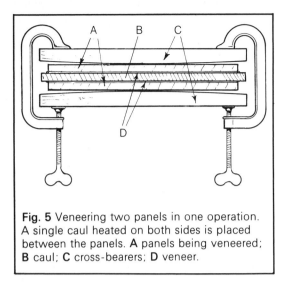

Fig. 5 Veneering two panels in one operation. A single caul heated on both sides is placed between the panels. **A** panels being veneered; **B** caul; **C** cross-bearers; **D** veneer.

the edges as shown in Fig. 4. Otherwise it would be awkward to apply the handscrews, since it would mean lifting up the bearers.

Small cauls can be heated before a fire or over a gas ring, but for large ones a shaving blaze is the most satisfactory. It gives out great heat and has the advantage that the heat is spread over the entire surface instead of just locally, as when a gas ring is used. Both sides of the caul should be heated, because it must be hot right through. Wood does not retain its heat very well, and it is obviously important that it does not chill before the entire cramping down is completed.

When thoroughly hot the caul is carried rapidly to the job and laid over the newspaper. The centre cross-bearers are laid curved side downwards immediately above the centre lower ones, and a handscrew put on at each end. Fig. 2 shows how the curved shape of the bearers has the effect of forcing the glue out from the centre.

Afterwards the end bearers are cramped down in the same way. If properly done it will be found that the glue has been squeezed out all round. In every case remember that the centre cross-bearers must always be applied first, as in Fig. 1, so that the glue is driven outwards. Otherwise the glue may be imprisoned in the centre and prevent the veneer from being pressed down. After a couple

of hours or so the screws can be slackened, but it is advisable to leave the work between the bearers to minimize the warping tendency.

In larger work many more cross-bearers have to be provided, and these are tightened in the same order, starting at the middle pair and working each way towards the ends.

When both sides of a panel have to be veneered, both should be pressed down in a single operation, using two cauls. The process is practically the same as that already described, but the operations have to be gone about speedily because the work cannot be prepared quite so conveniently. What happens is that the lower cross-bearers are laid across the trestles and the panel with its veneers in position placed handy. As soon as both cauls are hot, one is laid face upwards on the bearers, the groundwork and veneers placed above it, and the other caul on top. The cross-bearers are then handscrewed down as before.

In the case of two panels of about the same size having to be veneered on one side, a single caul can be placed between them, as shown in Fig. 5. The caul must be really hot right through because the heat is soon dissipated. Remember in all cases to place sheets of newspaper over the veneer. Unless this is done there is the risk of the latter sticking to the caul.

Resin glue. When resin glue of the cold-application type is being used there is not the same need for speed in the operation. The cauls are used cold—unless for some reason the work is needed urgently. In the latter case hot cauls are used, not to liquefy the glue, but to set it rapidly. However, it is not advisable for the inexperienced man to do this, as the whole procedure has to be carried out rapidly and with certainty because of the short time for adjustment. Once resin glue sets it cannot be reliquefied.

The use of resin glue carries certain advantages apart from the above. Little moisture is used, and consequently there is a minimum of swelling and subsequent shrinking and so less liability to cast, though there is always a certain risk when only one side of a panel is veneered. There is tremendous strength in resin glue and even unprotected edges are reasonably safe. For table tops it has the virtue of being resistant to both heat and damp.

It needs an even spread over both groundwork and veneer. In the trade a glue spreader is invariably used (see page 46), but for hand use, after brushing over the surface, it is advisable to use a hand spreader with serrated edge such as that in Fig. 6. No great thickness of glue is required but there must be no glue-starved places, hence the necessity for an even spread. Cramping is obviously necessary because resin has no natural tackiness. Fig. 7 shows the caul being cramped down when the veneer does not reach to the edges of the groundwork. Note the cross-bearers with curved edges.

Joints in veneers. When a joint has to be made

Fig. 6 (right) Spreader used for evening the glue over the groundwork.

Fig. 7 (below) Caul veneering showing the use of cross-bearers which have curved edges.

in the veneers of a panel to obtain the width, the jointing must be done before laying. The planing is done on the shooting-board, both pieces of veneer being shot at the same time. The veneer is fixed between a couple of pieces of wood with thumbscrews. The planing is virtually the same as in an ordinary joint. It can be tested against a straight-edge, though a man who is used to the work will be able to shoot the edge perfectly true without difficulty.

Assuming a long plane known to be accurate and

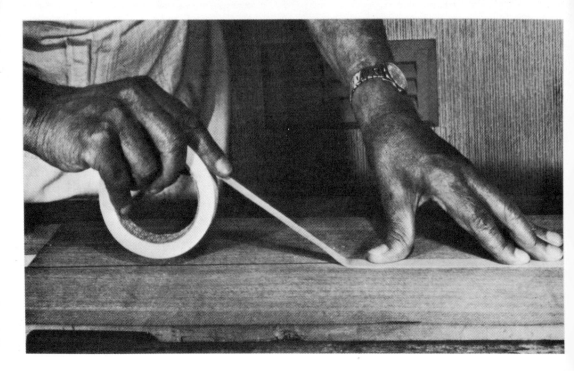

Fig. 8 (above) Taping a joint in veneer.

finely set is used, it is necessary only to plane at the centre until the plane ceases to remove shavings, and then take one or two shavings along the whole length. However, it is as well to use the straight-edge as a safeguard. After separating, the pieces are placed together in their correct relative positions and held together with gummed tape, as in Fig. 8. It is then treated as a single sheet and laid in the way already described with the tape away from the groundwork.

Chapter seven

Hammer veneering

Although the press and caul have largely super-seded hammer veneering there are still jobs for which the latter can be used with advantage. In the antique repair trade, for instance, it is still widely used. Furthermore few men in the small workshop have a press, and even for caul veneering it is necessary to have considerable equipment such as many cramps, large cauls, cross-bearers, and the facilities for heating large cauls.

There are some jobs, however, for which the hammer cannot be used. Marquetry, built-up patterns (except the simplest), veneers in which patches have been made are examples, the reason being that parts would be liable to move out of position. Furthermore the veneer would be liable to swell owing to the moisture involved in the operation, and subsequently to shrink, causing joints to open or possibly overlap.

It will be seen later that the principle of hammer veneering, so far as built-up patterns are concerned, is different from that of caul-veneering. In the latter the pattern is made up first and then laid as a whole. The reverse takes place in hammer veneering, the veneers being laid to overlap and the joints cut afterwards. Consequently only comparatively simple built-up patterns are suitable for laying with the hammer. In a straightforward pattern with, say, a cross-banding around the edge or plain bands running across, there is no difficulty. In fact, there is an advantage in laying cross-bandings with the hammer because, as the cutting gauge is used on the actual panel for cutting away the surplus veneer around the edges enabling the cross-banding to be added, the width of the latter is bound to be the same all round. Many workers, even when they lay the main part of a panel with a caul, often put down the cross-banding with the hammer afterwards for this reason. It is specially desirable when the banding is extra narrow.

The hammer can be used effectively for shaped work providing that the curve is not too acute. Quick curves create difficulty, especially when the grain of the veneer runs round the curve rather than across it. This is dealt with in greater detail in the chapter on shaped work.

The veneering hammer. The tool chiefly used is the veneering hammer, with which the surplus

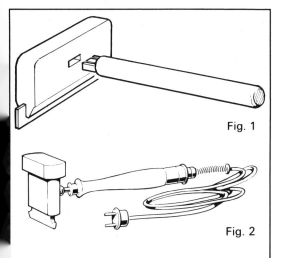

Fig. 1 The veneering hammer. Stock is about 15cm. (6in.) long, and handle about 25cm. (10in.).

Fig. 2 Electric veneering hammer.

glue is forced out. The cabinet-maker invariably makes his own hammer because it is so simple. Details of one are given in Fig. 1. There is no need to follow the sizes closely; a slight variation will make little or no difference. A saw-cut is made in the lower edge of the main stock to receive a piece of brass. To prevent the latter from cutting into or tearing the veneer the lower edge is rounded over with a file and then glasspapered. It could be about 1·5mm. ($\frac{1}{16}$in.) thick. Glue alone will hold it in position if it is a tight fit and the surfaces are roughened. If it should be inclined to work loose a little Epoxy resin glue can be used. The handle is fixed with a through-tenon joint wedged at the outside. Hardwood is advisable, because a fair pressure has to be applied.

An electrically heated hammer is also used some-times, this being plugged in. An example is shown in Fig. 2. The enlarged part at the opposite side to the pressing edge is used to heat the glue under the veneer.

A flat-iron, glue, a can of hot water, a swab, and some strips of gummed tape for sticking over joints are the only other requirements. The ordinary household flat-iron does quite well for the purpose, though nowadays an electric iron is generally used. Note that it cannot be used afterwards for laundry work.

A practical example

Preliminary work. To take a practical example, we are assuming that a panel about 90cm. (3ft.) by 50cm. (20in.) is to be veneered, the whole surface having to be covered completely. The panel or groundwork is prepared as described in Chapter two, the surface being made perfectly true and toothed all over. The veneer is cut about 10mm. ($\frac{3}{8}$in.) larger all round; if a sufficiently large leaf is not available, two pieces should match as closely as possible.

The glue. Good Scotch glue is used which should be made up fresh. Glue which has been heated up many times loses much of its virtue. It should be entirely free from lumpiness and all foreign matter. Once it is hot the brush should be raised a few inches from the pot, when the glue should flow down freely without breaking up into drops.

Fig. 3 (top) Use of electric iron to heat glue.

Fig. 4 (above) Using the veneering hammer.

The consistency is important because thick glue cannot be pressed out easily and thin glue soaks into the grain and is not so strong. Remember in this connection that, as a certain amount of dampness has to be applied to the outside of the veneer, some of it soaks through and is liable to thin out the glue still more. When light veneers such as sycamore, maple, satinwood, and so on are veneered, white glue should be used to prevent discoloration. This is made by the addition of a little flake white powder to the glue.

Both the groundwork and the underside of the veneer are well glued all over. Take the utmost care to see that there is no grit of any kind and that dust does not settle. It does not matter if the glue chills because it is heated with the iron later. Now place the veneer glued side downward and press down roughly all over with the hands

With the swab lightly damp about one half of the surface. This is to prevent the veneer from being scorched and to enable the iron to travel easily. On no account swamp the surface with water. Actually the less used the better, because it weakens the glue and causes the veneer to swell unduly. Remember that it is the moisture that is the chief cause of casting, and the less used the better the chance of keeping the work flat.

Using the veneering hammer. The flat-iron should be just hot enough to soften the glue; too much heat causes it to burn and deteriorate. Furthermore an over-heated iron causes steam to be generated, and this softens the veneer, making it more liable to stretch when the hammer is used, and subsequently shrink with increased liability to pull the work hollow. When the iron is held a few centimetres from the cheek a slight warmth should be felt. Wipe the sole with a rag and pass the iron back and forth across the damped half of the work as shown in Fig. 3. With the hammer proceed to squeeze out the surplus glue, working the former with a zig-zag movement from the centre to the edges as in Fig. 4. It is immaterial whether the hammer is held in one hand or whether two are used. A firm pressure is needed, but not so much as to break the veneer.

Work along the grain, because if the hammer is taken across it there is a tendency to stretch the veneer. This is particularly undesirable because t means that subsequent shrinkage is increased, with consequent casting of the work.

Special care is needed when the edge is reached because the hammer is liable to drop down and break the overhanging veneer. A good plan is to hold the hammer at an angle, as in Fig. 5, so that one corner overhangs and work it along parallel with the edge. If for any reason it is necessary to go over the work a second time a further damping s required, but avoid using more dampness than s essential. Excessive moisture makes the veneer swell, with increased liability to shrink as the moisture dries out. It is better to complete the pressing down in one operation if possible, because, apart from having to use more water, heating the glue again tends to make it deteriorate.

When one half is finished the other is damped and pressed out in the same manner. In the ordinary

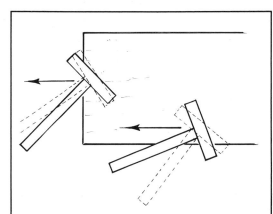

Fig. 5 How hammer is used at the edges.

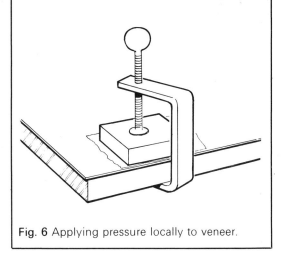

Fig. 6 Applying pressure locally to veneer.

way the whole thing will go down flat without any difficulty. To test it the finger-nails are tapped lightly over the surface, when a solid feeling should be apparent. Where there are any bubbles the part can be heated again locally and the hammer worked over it. Occasionally it happens that the veneer still rises, and then a block of wood must be heated and fixed down with a thumbscrew, as in Fig. 6. A piece of newspaper beneath prevents it from adhering. If the bubble is near the middle of the panel the block must be pressed down with bearers, as in Fig. 7.

Sometimes the veneer can be prevented from rising by laying a block of cold metal over it—an iron plane for instance. The cold metal chills the glue and makes it set rapidly. If the glue is already cold it must be heated first.

The overhanging edges of the veneer can be cut off straightway, as shown in Fig. 8. The panel is laid face side downwards upon a couple of battens, one of which projects at the edge to be cut. Press firmly down so that the veneer is forced against the batten and cut away the veneer with a keen chisel. The ends should be cut first so that if the corners should be split away the second cut *with* the grain removes the split portion. The panel should be laid face downwards to dry, and it is a good plan to damp the back to minimise warping. Always wipe over the surface with the swab well wrung out to remove any glue.

Making a joint. When a joint in the veneer has to be made, one sheet should be laid so that it overlaps the other by about 25mm. (1in.). A straight-edge is laid along the overlap and pressed tightly down. A thin, keen chisel or knife is drawn along the straight-edge so that it cuts through both thicknesses, as at Fig. 9A. Exert a fair pressure so that only one cut is needed because a second cut may tend to drift and cause a bad joint. At the same time do not cut too deeply into the groundwork, because this may cause a slight depression later as the glue shrinks. In the case of extra long joints it is advisable to fix the straight-edge with a couple of thumb-screws as shown.

The one strip of waste of the upper veneer Y can now be peeled away. Then by raising the veneer the waste strip beneath Z can be removed, as shown at C. Allow the veneer to drop back again, heat it with the iron, and press down firmly with the hammer. To prevent any tendency for the joint to open as it dries out, a length of gummed tape can be stuck over it. Fig. 10 shows the lower strip of waste veneer being removed.

Dealing with end grain. It was noted in Chapter two that, when a groundwork of softwood is used, it is necessary first to size it before the veneer is laid to prevent it from soaking up too

Fig. 7 Applying pressure at centre of panel.

Fig. 8 (bottom left) Trimming overhanging veneer.

Fig. 9 Stages in making a joint when hammer veneering. **A** knife worked along straight edge **X**, cutting through both thicknesses; **B** upper waste strip **Y** peeled away; **C** veneer raised to enable lower waste strip **Z** to be removed.

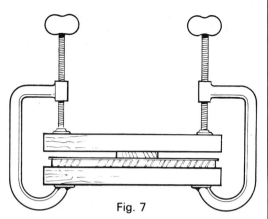

Fig. 7

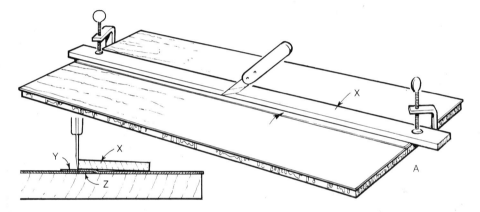

Fig. 9

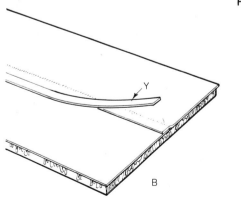

B

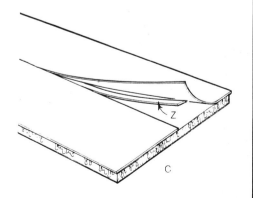

C

much of the glue. The same thing applies when end grain is being veneered. This is not a very satisfactory job in any case, but sizing does help. Several applications should be given, each being allowed to dry out before the next is applied. An example of veneering end grain is the case of a panel such as a table-top which is not clamped.

In some cases it is possible to avoid it by applying an edging, the grain of which runs crosswise, as shown in Fig. 11. The cross grain prevents a possible split in the panel in the event of shrinkage. The edging, of course, is applied before the face veneer is laid. If it can be tongued on or let into a groove, as at B, so much the better. Veneer can then be laid over this with safety.

Cross-banding. When a panel is to have a cross-banding, as in Fig. 12, the main sheet should be cut so that it stands in a trifle from the edge instead of overhanging. The reason for this is that the margin is gauged round and the veneer trimmed away immediately after laying, the glue being still soft. The gauge can be run around the edges, there being no overhang to hamper the fence. This is shown in Fig. 13. Fig. 14 shows the cross-banding being pressed down with the cross-peen of the hammer. Note the gummed tape stuck over the joints to prevent their opening as the moisture dries out.

Precautions against warping. It has already been noted that veneering both sides of a panel is the best safeguard against warping. There are jobs, however, where this may not be desirable. An example is a reproduction Queen Anne table-top. These old table-tops were veneered on the top only, and a reproduction should be treated similarly. When fixed to the framework the top is pulled flat, but the veneering has to be done before fixing, and to help matters it is an advantage to screw a series of stout battens to the underside, as in Fig. 15. These are screwed on before veneering, and they keep the whole thing flat during the drying out. They should be left on as long as possible—several days at least—and when taken off the top should straightway be screwed to its framework.

In some instances this cannot be done because

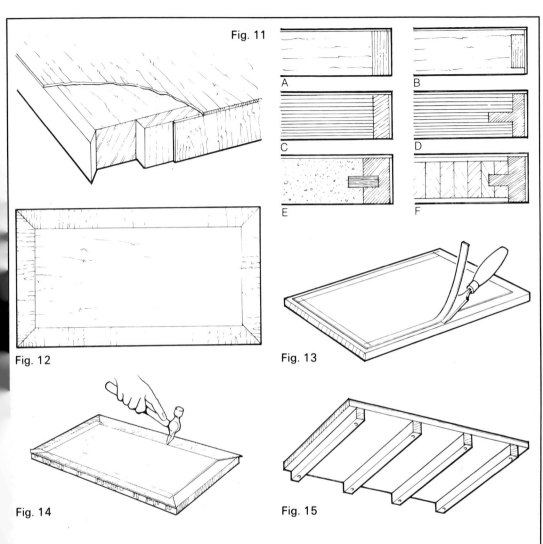

Fig. 11

A

B

C

D

E

F

Fig. 12

Fig. 13

Fig. 14

Fig. 15

Fig. 10 (bottom left) The lower strip of veneer being peeled away.

Fig. 11 Dealing with end grain edges.
A cross-grain strip applied and veneered;
B cross-grain strip set in groove; C plywood with applied strip; D tongued strip fitted to plywood; E chipboard with strip having loose tongue; F tongued edging fitted to lamin board.

Fig. 12 Cross-banded panel showing the corners mitred together.

Fig. 13 Removing waste when cross-banding. The veneer is short of the overall size so that the cutting gauge can be used around the edges.

Fig. 14 Pressing down cross-banding with the hammer.

Fig. 15 Battens screwed to underside of panel veneered on one side only.

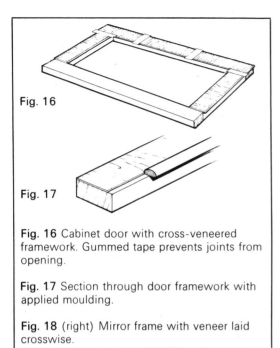

Fig. 16

Fig. 17

Fig. 16 Cabinet door with cross-veneered framework. Gummed tape prevents joints from opening.

Fig. 17 Section through door framework with applied moulding.

Fig. 18 (right) Mirror frame with veneer laid crosswise.

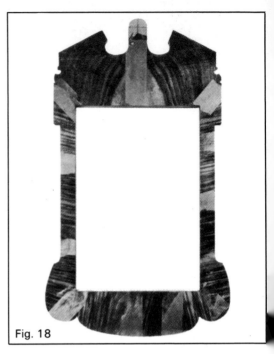

Fig. 18

the screw holes may be undesirable, in which case the panel should be cramped between pairs of battens. These are left on as long as possible. Matters can also be helped by damping the back of the groundwork. Remember also to have the iron only warm enough to heat the glue so that steam is avoided, and to work the hammer in the direction of the grain as far as possible, not across it, thus avoiding stretching the veneer and subsequent shrinkage.

Cross-veneering. A somewhat different kind of job for which the hammer is also useful is for door frames which are cross-veneered. In this the door is framed up in the usual way and is fitted and toothed. A number of strips of veneer are cut across the grain of a width sufficient to overhang the rails at both sides. They can be cut with the gauge (see page 34). On the shooting-board plane both ends of the pieces square so that they will make a close fit. With the hammer rub down one piece, and scrape away the glue squeezed out at the end. Fit the next piece up to it, rub down, and stick a piece of gummed tape over the joint, as in Fig. 16. It will be noticed

that the veneers butt up against each other at the corner joints. This was frequently done in Queen Anne work, though sometimes mitres were used. Note that the butt joints should line up with the actual joints of the framework.

When an applied moulding has to be fitted to the inner edge as shown in the section in Fig. 17, the veneer should stand in slightly at the inside instead of overhanging, because a gauge can then be run round immediately after laying to remove the waste in the margin. If this is not done it means trimming down afterwards. The first method is much simpler. The corners have to be cut with a chisel because the gauge cannot reach right in.

It should be noted that mouldings should never be fixed over veneer when it can possibly be avoided because the entire strain of a sudden jar on the moulding is taken by the veneer and it may be forced up. It is far better to cut away the veneer to form a sort of rebate, as in Fig. 17, so that the moulding is fixed direct to the solid wood. Furthermore, it gives a definite fixing line.

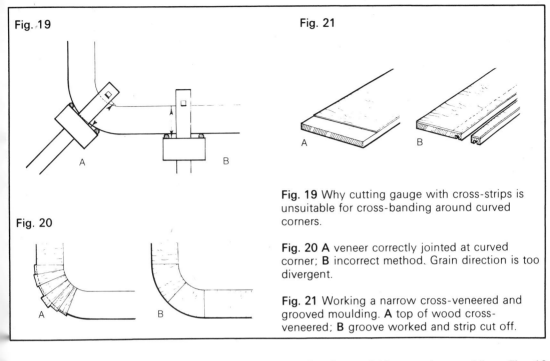

Fig. 19

Fig. 20

Fig. 21

A   B

A   B

A   B

Fig. 19 Why cutting gauge with cross-strips is unsuitable for cross-banding around curved corners.

Fig. 20 A veneer correctly jointed at curved corner; **B** incorrect method. Grain direction is too divergent.

Fig. 21 Working a narrow cross-veneered and grooved moulding. **A** top of wood cross-veneered; **B** groove worked and strip cut off.

When the framing has to be moulded in the solid as distinct from having an applied moulding, the difficulty is that the moulding has to be worked before the framework is assembled, consequently the glue used in veneering would be liable to run down over the moulding and it would be difficult to clean it off afterwards. One way is to prepare the parts as though there were to be no veneering, and assemble the whole dry as far as the uncut moulding will allow. The joints can then be levelled, the parts veneered, the moulding worked, and the mitres cut. When assembled the joints should be level and need only be scraped.

Alternatively the jointing, rebating, and moulding are completed. The moulding is then French polished or lacquered, the mitres cut, and the whole assembled. After levelling the surface is veneered, the inner edge of the veneer being planed straight. The latter is kept level with the moulding. A certain amount of glue will be squeezed out over the moulding but this can be cleaned away immediately with a damp rag and a pointed stick of wood. The polish will prevent any surplus from sticking to the moulding. Fig. 18 shows a mirror frame with the veneer laid cross-wise, all joints being taped.

Shaped cross-banded corners. When a cross-banding has to be taken around a rounded corner there is a slight difficulty as the gauge is liable to wobble about. When completely circular shapes are being gauged the usual plan is to fit a fence having the two cross strips shown in Fig. 19, because then the gauge, having two bearings, can be held steady. It will be seen on reflection that this cannot be done in the present case because the width of the cross-band would vary in the straight and curved portions. This is made clear in Fig. 19.

The best plan is to use the ordinary cutting gauge, holding it as steady as possible, and to finish off with a flat gouge or a knife drawn around the curve. When the waste has been peeled away the pieces for the corners can be fitted as at Fig. 20A. It is advisable to use several small pieces rather than just one or two, because in the latter case the joints become very obvious owing to the

Fig. 22 (right) Clockcase veneered with walnut curls. The domed top is made from shaped pieces veneered and the mitred round (see also page 103). Made by the author.

difference in grain direction being so strongly marked (see Fig. 20B). Each piece will have to be slightly hollowed at the inner edge to take the curve. The usual plan is to glue all the parts together first and then fit it as a whole to the corner.

Veneered moulding. Some mouldings are cross-veneered, and they are usually obtained ready-made. If the reader wishes to make them himself he should use either a shaped caul or a sandbag. In some cases mouldings are entirely flat and the simplest way of making these is to cross-veneer a length of stuff as at Fig. 21A. The groove for the bar (if wanted) is then worked in the underside and the strip slit away as at B. It is mitred up as though it were a length of ordinary moulding.

Sometimes the large members of cornice and similar mouldings have to be veneered. An example is the rounded member of the clockcase bracket on page 103. When a spindle moulder is available a reverse caul can be made and used, but this would be difficult by hand methods, and the alternative is to use a sandbag, this being

Fig. 22

heated and the work pressed into it. When this is not available a simple way is to use a contact adhesive. This is described more fully in Chapter twelve.

Chapter eight

Cleaning up veneer

Although it is possible to plane a veneered surface, unless one has had considerable experience it is a risky business owing to the liability of the grain to tear out. By setting a smoothing plane with a high-pitched cutter very fine and placing the back iron almost touching the cutting edge, some cabinet makers can clean up a veneer of burr walnut, and it has the advantage of making the surface dead true. For the man with limited experience, however, the safer plan is to use the scraper only.

It is for this reason that any surface glue should be wiped off as far as possible after veneering. Glue clogs the scraper easily. The same thing applies to any paper or gummed tape, which should be damped to allow easy peeling off. When the work has to be machine sanded it is essential that all glue and paper are removed, because there is no preliminary scraping and the rapid clogging of the sanding belt soon prevents it from doing its work; it may even result in indentations being formed owing to the glue heaping up and bearing on the veneer. It is to save the lengthy job of removing the gummed tape that the glue jointer for veneer is used. In hand work a great deal of laborious scraping can be avoided by wiping the surface as free as possible from glue, or by damping any paper and peeling it off.

Using the scraper. Plain straight-grained veneers present no special difficulties, but in awkward grain it is advisable to hold the scraper at an angle so that it takes more of a slicing cut. The same thing applies to cross-banding, marquetry, and built-up patterns in which the direction of the grain varies a great deal. Fig. 1 shows the scraper in use. It seems unnecessary to add that care has to be taken not to scrape down too much locally, because there is a strict limit to the amount of wood that can be removed since the veneer is necessarily thin. Holding the scraper at an angle is essential when starting a cut at the near end; it enables one end of the scraper to be actually on the wood at the start of the cut.

When scraping is completed a thorough scouring with glasspaper follows. No. 2 Fine can be used

Fig. 1 (left) How the scraper is held when cleaning veneer. In some cases it is held askew to minimize tearing out.

first (except for such fine woods as burr walnut, amboyna, and so on), this being followed by No. 1½ or No. 1. When possible, the glasspapering should be in the same direction as the grain, but this is not always practicable. For example, in a cross-banded panel the grain of the banding at the sides is at right angles to that of the main panel, and here it is best to ignore the banding and to finish off with a very fine grade glasspaper. The same thing applies to built-up patterns and marquetry.

Awkward grain. Some woods have no definite direction of grain—burr walnut, for example—and the best plan here is to use a paper no coarser than No. 0 and to work the rubber with a circular movement, finishing off with Flour grade paper. In every case a cork rubber should be used. Avoid dubbing over the edges, because it may work right through the veneer, apart from producing an unsightly result. After all surfaces and edges have been papered, the rubber with a piece of No. 1 paper on it should be passed once lightly over the edges at an angle so that the extreme sharpness is taken off. One last

note is that glasspaper which has been used to clean up, say, mahogany should not be used on light woods, because it is liable to cause discoloration.

The orbital sander. For work having varied grain direction as in built-up panels, cross-banding, marquetry, etc., an invaluable machine is the orbital sander. It can be obtained as an individual hand-operated machine or as an attachment for an electric drill. Its disc does not rotate but moves as a whole in a small circle of about 2mm. (⅛in.) diameter. The best way of visualizing its movement is to think of a pencil dot marked in any position on the pad. When the machine is set in movement the dot moves in a tiny circle. Thus all the grains of the abrasive move simultaneously in small circles, and there is no definite direction to the path of the abrasive. Fig. 2 shows it in use.

Incidentally, allow as much time as possible after

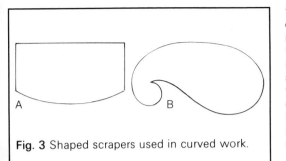

Fig. 3 Shaped scrapers used in curved work.

veneering before cleaning up. This enables any sinking to take place. Otherwise the sinking may occur some time after the job has been finished. Forty-eight hours is a minimum for built-up panels. If a week can be allowed so much the better.

Machine sanding. This is the method used in the machine shop, and there are various types of machines. An important point is to avoid glue on the surface as far as possible because of its liability to clog the sanding belt. For the same reason any tape on the surface should be cleaned off first. If it is sanded off there is not only the clogging tendency, but also a liability of the joints to heat up. It is because of this that tapeless jointers are frequently preferred. Note that only the belt-type of sander is suitable, and care must be taken not to work too locally. Even though the sanding may not go right through the veneer, it may make it so thin as to be unreliable. Disc sanders are quite unsuitable because the circular path of the glasspaper shows up as a defect, and in any case is liable to cause unevenness in tone in subsequent staining.

Shaped work. Curves of plain convex shape can generally be cleaned up with the ordinary straight scraper. The same applies to concave shapes unless the curve is very acute or when the grain of the veneer runs crosswise to the curve. In the former case it may be necessary to use glasspaper only, this being wrapped around a shaped wood rubber. An example of this is given on page 64. where the curved edges are veneered. The large curves could be scraped but the small concave shapes need to be cleaned with glasspaper wrapped round a wood rubber. Cross-grained, concave shapes may call for the use of a shaped scraper as at Fig. 3A, and it will probably have to be filed to shape, the curved being slightly quicker than that of the workpiece.

Compound curvature is more difficult and the use of a curved scraper is inevitable when the shape is hollow. The scraper at Fig. 3B is useful in that its varying shape enables it to be used on curvature of irregular form. In any case it is followed by glasspaper held on a shaped rubber, and the direction in which the latter is used depends upon the grain direction. It should follow the grain as far as possible, but in many cases this is impossible because the veneers used in compound shapes have to be tailored to enable them to fit around the shape, and as a result the grain direction may vary widely. In this case nothing coarser than No. 1 should be used at the start, followed by No. 0 and Flour grade.

An example of compound curvature is the vase, Fig. 11, page 105. This was largely cleaned up on the lathe. All gummed tape was removed and any obvious surface glue scraped off. The same thing applied to any joints which were not quite level. A flat scraper was used. Finally the lathe was set in motion at its lowest speed and glasspaper used, No. 1 followed by No. 0 and finally Flour grade. Similar work which could not be put in the lathe would have to be scraped then glass-papered by hand. Sometimes the glasspaper would be held in the hand only, but towards the edges a rubber would be desirable to prevent their being dubbed over. Anything like a reverse rubber might be impracticable owing to the varying curvature.

Chapter nine

Built-up patterns 1

In the modern shop equipped with a press, built-up patterns are invariably pieced together, made up as a complete unit, and laid as a whole in the press, because, apart from any other advantage, it is the quickest method. In the hand shop, too, it is generally an advantage to use the caul, though straightforward patterns can be laid with the hammer. The door of the simple cabinet in Fig. 1 is an elementary piece of work which could be laid with either the hammer or the caul. The patterns in Fig. 2 also lend themselves to either method, though if the grain has to be matched closely the caul method is the better.

More elaborate patterns, however, are best cauled because of the awkwardness of cutting the intricate joints on the job itself. It will be realized that, when the hammer is used, it is impossible to cut the joints before laying the veneer because the damping and heating inevitably cause the veneer to stretch and contract, the effect of which would be to spoil the joints. It is necessary to lay the veneers with their edges overlapping and cut through both thicknesses with the chisel, and this, as already stated, would be a difficult job in intricate patterns. In many cases it would be altogether impracticable.

Sometimes a compromise is advisable. Take for instance a large built-up panel with a narrow cross-banding around the edge. To make up the whole of this in the veneer, including the narrow cross-banding, would, though possible, be somewhat awkward, because if the veneer were made perfectly square and the panel were the merest trifle out, the whole of the inaccuracy would fall on the narrow banding, which would consequently taper towards one corner. For this reason the usual plan in the hand shop is to caul down the whole of the centre part of the pattern as one, and then lay the cross-banding with the hammer afterwards. As the cutting gauge is run round the edge to enable the waste to be peeled away to make room for the cross-banding, the latter is bound to be parallel. This is not done in large veneering shops, where the usual plan is to make the whole thing a trifle full all round to allow for trimming.

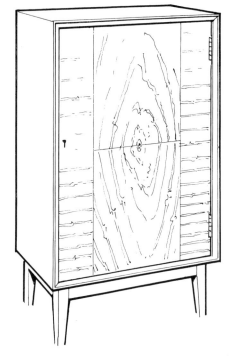

Fig. 1 (left) Cabinet with door having a simple built-up pattern.

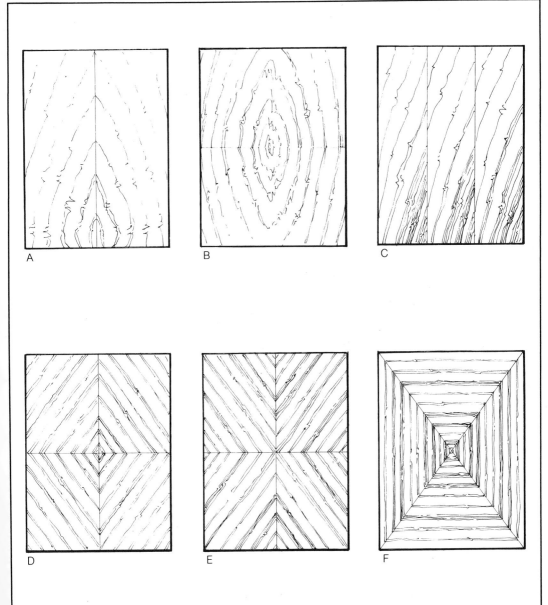

Fig. 2 Matched patterns in veneer. **A** book-matched; **B** butt-matched; **C** running matches; **D** diamond; **E** reverse diamond; **F** diagonal quartered. Simple patterns as **A** and **B** could be hammer-veneered, the joints being cut with chisel and straight-edge during the laying process. However, it is more satisfactory to assemble the veneers beforehand, holding the parts together with gummed tape, and lay by the caul method or in the press.

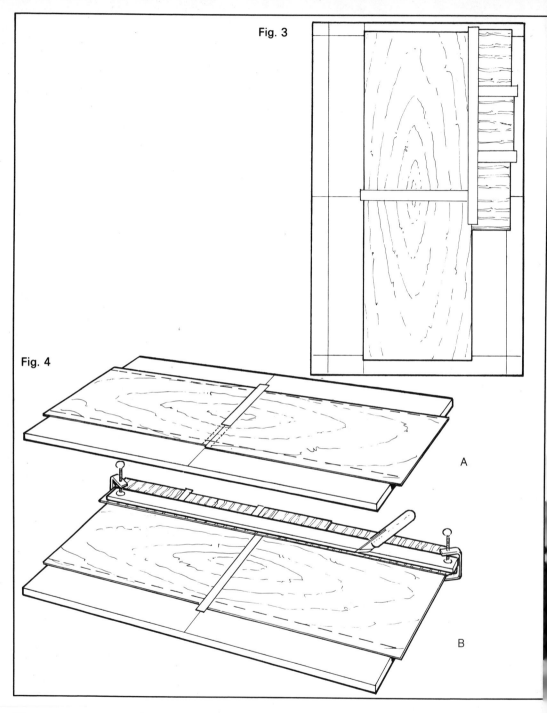

Fig. 3

Fig. 4

A

B

72

Fig. 3 Assembly of the veneers required for the door of the cabinet in **Fig. 1** when the caul or press is used.

Fig. 4 Laying the veneers of the cabinet door in **Fig. 1** by the hammer method.

Simple built-up pattern. The door of the cabinet in Fig. 1 may be taken as an example of a simple built-up pattern. A panel of laminated board or multi-ply would make a reliable groundwork, better than solid wood because of the width which might eventually cause a gap to appear at the closing edge due to shrinkage. It should be fitted to the cabinet and prepared as described in Chapter two.

Although either the caul method or the hammer could be used, the former would be the simpler, though it would need a large number of cramps and a caul slightly larger than the door itself. We deal first with the caul method. It will be understood that if a press were available this would be used, the procedure for preparing the work being identical. For the centre part two consecutive leaves of figured veneer are needed, and these would be fitted together on a flat board and a strip of gummed tape stuck over the joint. The lines of all the joints would be drawn in pencil on the board as a guide to assembling as in Fig. 3, though on so simple a pattern it is not essential. The joint itself is planed true on the shooting board (see page 34). After assembling the sides of these, figured veneers have to be cut straight and trimmed true. The edges can be planed before the two veneers are fitted together, but even so it will probably be necessary to take a final skim where the two pieces adjoin. Incidentally, if the veneers are at all buckled they should be flatted first as described on page 41.

The plain straight-grained flanking pieces follow, and jointing is unavoidable over such a length of cross-grain. Either each whole length can be assembled and held together with gummed tape and the inner edge trimmed straight afterwards; or, rather more simply, the separate pieces can be added individually as in Fig. 3. It is simple to plane clean joints both where they adjoin the centre figured veneer and with each other. The whole being assembled in this way, it is laid on the groundwork, care being taken to centre the whole

correctly using centre lines. It will be realized that the veneer overhangs the groundwork all round, and this overhang is trimmed away after the glue has set. The method of laying is dealt with in Chapter six.

For those who prefer to use the hammer method which avoids the necessity for many cramps and a caul, the two matched figured centre veneers are laid first. A centre line is drawn first across the groundwork and one veneer put down with an overlap at the line of about 10mm. ($\frac{3}{8}$in.). The second is laid in the same way again with the overlap and a straight-edge cramped down level with the centre line. A keen chisel or knife is drawn along it to cut through both thicknesses and the top waste piece peeled away. To reach the lower waste piece the veneer will have to be raised (see Chapter seven), after which the joint is rubbed down with the hammer. It may be necessary to reheat the glue first with the flat iron. Gummed tape stuck over the joint will prevent it from opening as the moisture dries out. (Fig. 4).

Either of two methods could be followed for the straight-grained flanking veneers. In the first the sides of the figured veneers should be cut straight with the knife and straight-edge as shown by the dotted lines at Fig. 4A, and the straight-grained veneers fitted up individually, gummed tape being stuck over the joints.

In the second method the veneers would be jointed together as a whole and laid with an overlap of about 10mm. ($\frac{3}{8}$in.) over the centre veneers. A straight-edge cramped down as at Fig. 4B enables a cut to be made through both thicknesses, after which the waste is peeled away as before. This second method would be used when the flanking veneers are fairly wide.

All told the use of the caul is the more satisfactory method, but whichever is followed any compensating veneer at the back should be put down at the same time. In caul veneering both back and front are laid simultaneously with two cauls. When the hammer is used the back veneer is laid immediately after the front without any drying interval. In this way the pull of the front veneer is equalized by that at the back.

The quartered panels Fig. 2 D, E, F, are best laid

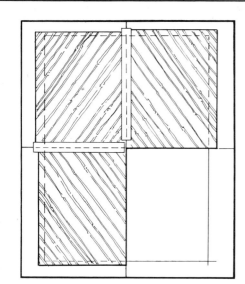

Fig. 5

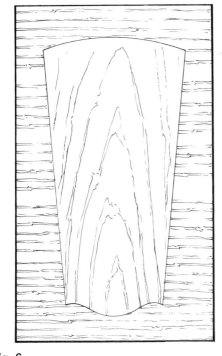

Fig. 6

with the caul. Consecutive veneers from the pack are fitted together on a flat board on which centre lines have been drawn. Cut out the veneers to size with chisel and straight-edge, starting the cut where the grain is short. In this way splintering out is avoided. Trim the edges on the shooting-board (see page 34) and when close joints have been made stick strips of gummed tape over them to hold the whole together (see Fig. 5).

A design suitable for caul veneering is shown in Fig. 6. Here again the use of both figured and plain veneers provides an interesting contrast. Begin by drawing out the pattern on a flat board as in Fig. 7, and prepare two templates in thin hardwood of the top and bottom shapes. Place a length of straight-grained veneer at the top and hold it in position with one or two pieces of gummed tape. Put the figured veneer in position to overlap the other and again use gummed tape. Note that the template is made about 2mm. ($\frac{1}{8}$in.) oversize at each end, but with marks of the finished size made on it as in Fig. 7.

With the special knife (see page 37) make a cut through both thicknesses. It does not matter if the knife overruns at the ends. The unwanted pieces are lifted away and the ends of the plain veneer cut away level with the top corners. The lower shape is dealt with in the same way. The figured veneer and top and bottom plain veneers are now in position and the sloping sides have to be cut. The straight-edge is held level with the corners and the cut made with the knife, see left, Fig. 8. Both sides being cut the side veneers are fitted individually as at the right hand side, Fig. 8.

It will be realized that constructed in this way the top and bottom joints are level with the corners. Since these joints are in line with the grain they scarcely show, but if it is preferred to avoid joints level with the corners the method in Fig. 9 can be followed. Here the templates are cut to the actual extent of the curves, including the sloping ends. The cut through both thicknesses is made as

Fig. 5 Veneers of quartered panel fitted together.

Fig. 6 Design with interesting contrast of figured and plain veneers.

74

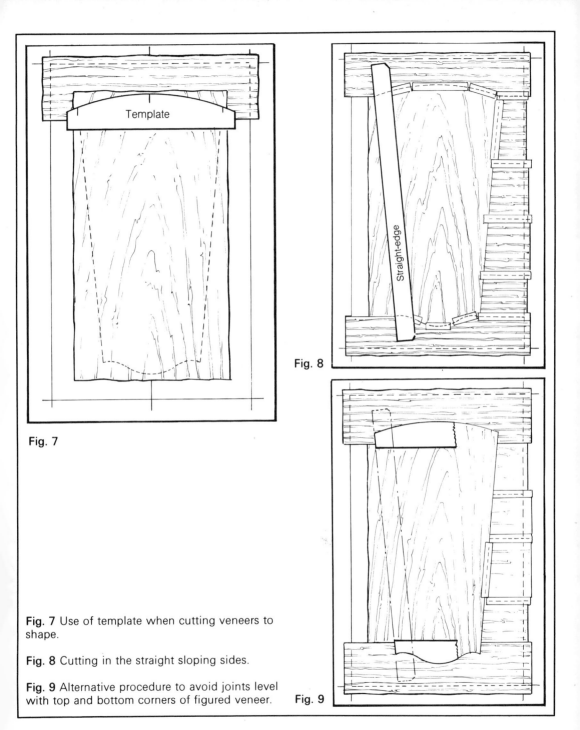

Template

Straight-edge

Fig. 7

Fig. 8

Fig. 9

Fig. 7 Use of template when cutting veneers to shape.

Fig. 8 Cutting in the straight sloping sides.

Fig. 9 Alternative procedure to avoid joints level with top and bottom corners of figured veneer.

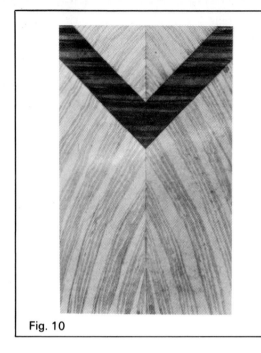

Fig. 10

before but care is taken not to overrun the ends. Afterwards the sloping cut with the straight-edge is made as before.

Another design. In Fig. 10 is another example of a built-up pattern in veneer which should preferably be made up for veneering with the caul or press. Incidentally, one advantage the caul method has is that in the event of a slip only one odd piece of veneer is spoilt, whereas a faulty cut with the knife when jointing on the groundwork using the hammer method may spoil the whole job.

In Fig. 10 there are two matched sheets jointed down the centre, these being consecutive leaves, and a V-shaped banding of dark wood let into it. A full-size drawing is the first necessity, this being prepared on a sheet of cartridge paper stretched on a flat board (see Fig. 12).

Flatting. If any of the veneers are cockled it is necessary to flat them otherwise it will be impossible to ensure accurate jointing. For plain grained veneer damp both sides with water using

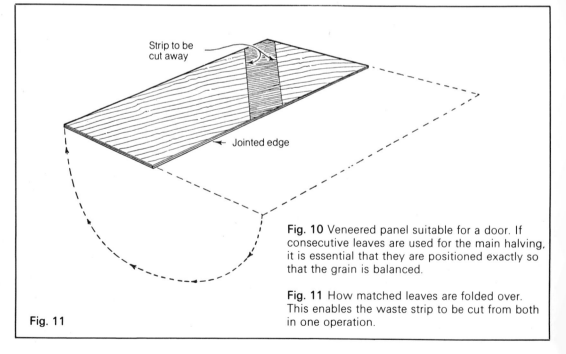

Strip to be cut away

Jointed edge

Fig. 11

Fig. 10 Veneered panel suitable for a door. If consecutive leaves are used for the main halving, it is essential that they are positioned exactly so that the grain is balanced.

Fig. 11 How matched leaves are folded over. This enables the waste strip to be cut from both in one operation.

Fig. 11A Corner cabinet with lower door veneered with curl mahogany. Photograph by courtesy of Waring & Gillow Ltd.

a swab, and cramp between hot cauls. After an hour or so the cramps can be removed, when the veneer should be used as soon as possible owing to a tendency to become buckled again. In difficult grain, such as African curls, etc., this treatment may be too harsh, and the better plan is to damp the veneers with thin glue size. If placed overnight between two flat boards with a weight above, the veneer should be flat and ready for use in the morning.

The halving. Use two consecutive sheets for the main halving and joint them, planing the joints on the shooting-board. Place them together in the exact positions and fold the one over as in Fig. 11. Make sure that the edges are perfectly level and cut away the strip to be occupied by the banding. If the veneer is tight for size a single cut could be made and the two pieces slid apart; a better effect is produced by cutting away the strip as the grain looks more natural. Use a keen chisel worked against a straight-edge and start at the jointed edge. Any splitting out at the completion of the cut then occurs at the outer edge which is trimmed away later. The straight-edge should be placed on the veneer to be used, not the waste strip, and a firm pressure should be maintained. Trim afterwards with the plane.

The two top pieces are now assembled on the drawing, care being taken to keep the joint central and the sides balanced as shown in Fig. 13. Drive in a couple of veneer pins at the waste at the edge and put a strip of gummed tape down the joint. A heavy weight at the lower end will prevent movement whilst the other parts are fitted.

The banding. Fig. 14 shows the next stage of adding this. It will be noticed that two joints are shown, but this is a matter that depends partly on the width of the veneer being used and partly upon the size of the work. The fewer the joints the better. The first piece to be fitted is that at the point of the V. Shoot the edge and place in position, keeping the edge horizontal. Tack down with a few pins through the waste edges and fit the other parts up to it. If the veneer is wide enough it may be an advantage to cut the V shape in the top edge as shown inset, so that it fits up to the top veneers. It needs clean cutting. Add the remaining pieces, making sure that the joints are close, and hold down with gummed tape as

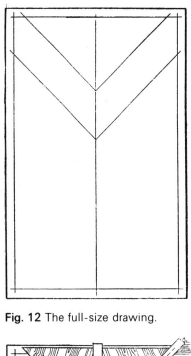

Fig. 12 The full-size drawing.

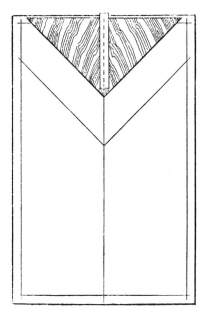

Fig. 13 Top halving assembled.

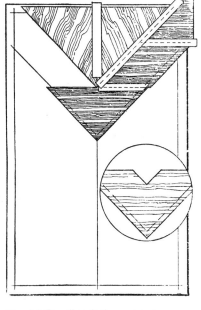

Fig. 14 Banding being added.

Fig. 15 Lower halving being fitted.

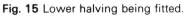

Fig. 16 Cross-banding a circular table edge.
After rubbing with the cross-peen of the hammer,
the veneer is held with pieces of cellulose tape.

shown. When completed mark the width of the banding and cut away the waste with chisel and straight-edge. Work the chisel *away* from the point of the V to avoid cracking away the tip. For the same reason place the straight-edge on the banding, not on the waste to be trimmed away. It may be desirable to trim the edges afterwards with the plane, but if cut cleanly it is not essential.

Lower veneers. Theoretically the two remaining veneers should make a good fit up to the banding and against each other. As a practical matter a shaving here and there is usually necessary. When all is accurate, stick gummed tape over the joints, and the whole is then ready for laying with the caul.

Hammer veneering. For those who prefer to use the hammer veneering method, the following is a brief description of the process. The two main halved veneers are laid, being jointed down the centre on the job. The V banding position is marked and a cut made about 6mm. ($\frac{1}{4}$in.) in on the *waste side* of each line. Now lay the banding veneer to cover the banding area with a generous allowance all round, letting it overlap the veneers already laid. With straight-edge and a thin knife cut right through both thicknesses, taking care to start the point of the V exactly on the joint and avoiding overrunning. Peel away the waste, raising the veneer to reach that beneath as in normal jointing, and rub down, taping all joints to prevent their opening as the glue sets. Although the work *can* be done with the hammer, the caul system is the more satisfactory for patterns of this kind because it tends to give a more accurate result as the work is not concealed by the overlap of the veneers.

Fig. 17 Mirror frame veneered with cross-banded walnut. Made by the author.

Fig. 18 Parts for the mirror frame shown above. They have been rebated and veneered and are ready for the veneer to be trimmed and the moulding worked.

Chapter ten

Built-up patterns 2

Fig. 1 shows a pair of doors with matched curls and cross-banded surround. As the latter is wide the whole thing can be made up complete before laying. The two matched curls are butted together, and when Scotch glue is used it is advisable to shoot the joint a trifle hollow because curls are liable to swell out at the centre when damped. If this is not done the ends of the joint may tend to open. When taping the joint the centre can be forced together. This will cause the veneer to buckle slightly but this flattens out when the caul is applied. In fact the application of glue usually brings the whole flat.

Fig. 2 shows the curls in position on the drawing, and Fig. 3 shows the cross-banding being added. Note that the corners are made up of two pieces each mitred together, and are fitted as a whole in position.

Other examples which may be mentioned under the heading of built-up panels are Fig. 4, 6, and 8,

Fig. 1 (below) Pair of decorative flush doors in walnut.

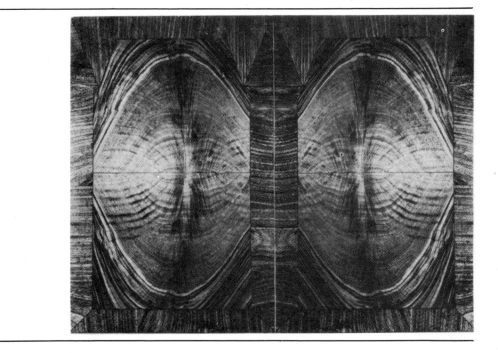

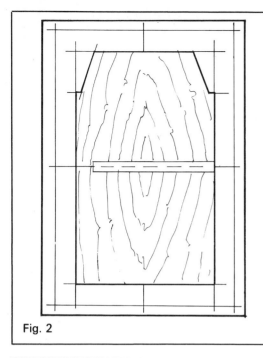

Fig. 2

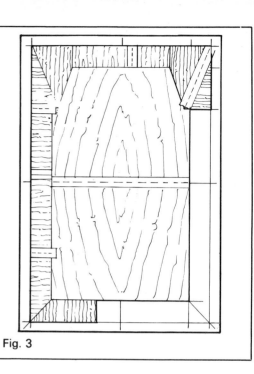

Fig. 3

Fig. 2 The centre curls trimmed to shape and in position.

Fig. 3 The cross-banding partly added.

Fig. 4 (below left) Panel with inset ring of contrasting wood.

though they are really plain panels with inset details. In some cases a metal template is needed, though for work having straight joints there is no necessity for it. In all the examples the background could be plain as shown or it could be halved or quartered.

In the case of Fig. 4 a template is the first necessity, and, being circular, it should if possible be turned on the lathe. If this is impracticable the shape should be scribed with dividers, carefully fretted with a metal-cutting fretsaw, and trued with file and glasspaper wrapped around a flat piece of wood. However, as there is always the chance of slight inaccuracy, two diameter lines at right angles should be scribed in, and one marked with an identification mark (say, **T** for top). Then when the

Fig. 5 Cutting round template with knife.

Fig. 5A (right) Simple mirror frame with cross-banded edging and halved pattern on the pediment. This piece made by the author.

sheets of veneer are cut the template can be held in the same relative position so that any inaccuracy occurs in the same position in both, ensuring a close fit. When the template is turned this is unnecessary, though the diameters may be needed to enable it to be centred. The thickness of the metal might be No. 16 gauge—about 1·5mm. ($\frac{1}{16}$in.)

Place the veneer on a flat board free from indentations, and mark upon the face the position of the design. Place the template in position, and hold it with two strips of gummed tape stuck across it at right angles. It is essential that the template is not moved whilst both inner and outer shapes are cut. Keep the knife close up to the template and take great care not to let it wander with the grain. It is

advisable to cut the inner ring first, and for this the special knife shown at 13B, page 37, is recommended because it works round the concave curve easily. The narrow point enables it to negotiate the quick curve easily and the wide blade ensures stiffness. For the outer curve the knife shown at Fig. 12, page 37, can be used.

Now cut the veneer for the inlay in the same way, again putting the work on a flat board. It should be realized that any indentations in the board will cause the knife to break right through and spoil the veneer. Fig. 5 shows the inlay veneer being cut. In practice the knife would be held rather near the point, but it is shown as it is to reveal the shape of the point.

If the veneers are now tried together it will be found that they will fit perfectly providing that the cutting has been accurate. Hold them together with strips of gummed tape. It is then merely a matter of laying the whole as though it were a single sheet of veneer. The caul or press should be used, and a sheet of paper should be placed between the veneer and the caul to prevent it from sticking.

Fig. 6 (top right) Diamond pattern inset into light background.

Fig. 7 (left) Pattern marked out. Note that the lines project beyond the points of the star.

Fig. 8 (above right) Pattern of interlacing discs.

A point to note is that all the veneers should be of the same thickness as otherwise the thin veneers will not receive full pressure. If there is a slight difference place several sheets of paper or a layer of felt over the veneer to take up the difference.

The star design in Fig. 6 can be cut entirely with straight-edge and knife. The veneer for the dark star shape is fixed down on the light veneer and held with gummed tape as in Fig. 7. On this are drawn the lines of the star shape in pencil. Note that in every case the pencil lines project beyond the points, the reason being that the knife can then be started in the exact position at the points. It will be realized that the straight-edge is bound to conceal

Fig. 9 Template used for cutting out, and shapes partly cut.

parts of the pencil lines, and unless the lines are projected it will be impossible to see exactly where to start the knife.

Hold the latter at a *slight* angle so that when cut out the star is a trifle larger than the opening in which it will fit. In this way the thickness of the cut is taken up. Care is needed at the points and internal angles not to chip away the short grain. It is often a help to stick a piece of gummed tape over such places as in Fig. 7 to prevent weak places from breaking away. Firm cuts are needed and they must penetrate both thicknesses. According to the woods used a second cut may be needed. Take special care at the start of the cuts, and avoid over-running at the end. When completed, interchange the pieces and hold the star in position with gummed tape. Lay with the caul or press.

The design in Fig. 8 looks more complicated than actually is. A template of the circular shape is needed, but if not specially made it can be any

circular metal item. In this case a lathe chuck was used as in Fig. 9, but providing the size is approximately right almost any item could be used. Alternatively, turn a hardwood template.

Square lines are drawn on the main background veneer to enable the design to be centred. The template is placed on one of the circle positions and a cut made round it. There is no need to cut all the way round the circle; only the main over-all outline shape need be cut. The process is repeated on the other two circles thus removing the trefoil shape shown in Fig. 9.

Circular shapes are now cut in three other veneers thus producing three discs. By placing one in position with the correct grain direction and over-lapping each adjoining disc in turn the extent of the two concave curves can be marked with a sharp pencil. These curves are now cut using the template as a guide. This leaves the four small centre pieces to be cut out with the template. Theoretically all should fit but in practice a certain amount of trim-ming or recutting may be needed. When assemb-ling, fit each piece to its neighbours and stick

85

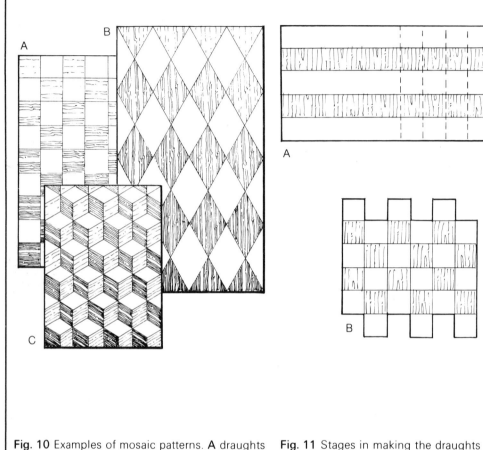

Fig. 10 Examples of mosaic patterns. **A** draughts board; **B** diamond; **C** cube.

Fig. 11 Stages in making the draughts board pattern.

gummed tape over the joints. A rub with the cross-peen of the hammer usually ensures their going together level.

Another way of doing the work is to use a keen carving gouge of the required curvature. It should be about 15mm. or 18mm. wide ($\frac{5}{8}$in. or $\frac{3}{4}$in.), and quite often the design is arranged to suit the curvature of the gouge. As the same gouge is used for all the parts a good fit should result. It is necessary to draw in the design on the background veneer using correctly centred compasses. These

centres are at the points of an equilateral triangle. To clear away the unwanted centre the trefoil shape is cut out with the gouge about 1mm. ($\frac{1}{25}$in.) inside the line. Then when the final cut is made right on the line the inner part will crumble away and there will be no liability for the wedge shape of the gouge to overrun the line. Similar precautions are taken when cutting the inset shapes, except that the preliminary cut is outside the line.

Built-up mosaic patterns. The simplest example of this is the draughts board pattern at Fig. 10A

86

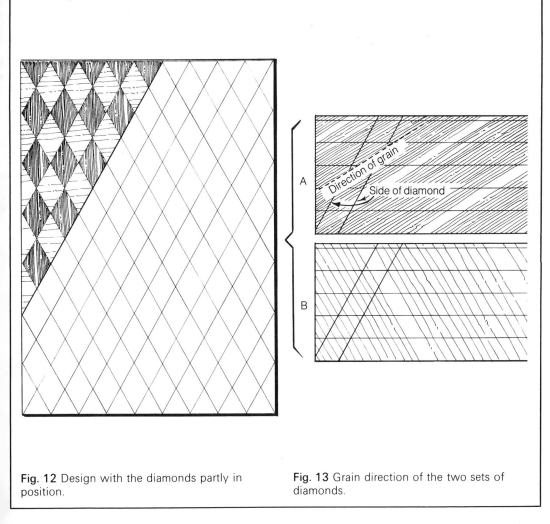

Fig. 12 Design with the diamonds partly in position.

Fig. 13 Grain direction of the two sets of diamonds.

Slightly more complicated is the diamond type B, and still more so the 'cube' form at C. A drawing is not essential for design A though some may prefer to prepare one as a check when assembling. Fig. 11 shows the procedure. Strips of veneer in two woods are cut out with the cutting gauge and assembled side by side as at Fig. 11A. Trim each edge on the shooting board before cutting, and also trim the gauged edge afterwards. Take care to keep the veneer the same way round for each strip as some woods appear lighter when viewed from one direction than from the other. For the same reason

keep the same side of the veneer uppermost. There should be an extra square in each strip because when they are assembled one square is lost as shown at Fig. 11B.

In the case of design B draw out the pattern on cartridge paper and prepare the veneer in strips, taking care to have the correct grain direction. Note that this direction runs through the centre of the diamonds as in Fig. 12 and does not align with the sides. It is a help to nail a guide to the shooting board at the required angle when trimming. Plane

Fig. 14

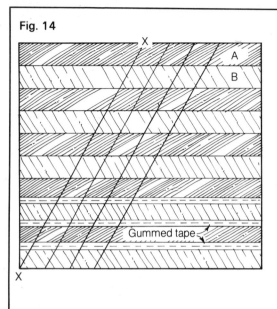

X

A

B

Gummed tape

X

Fig. 15

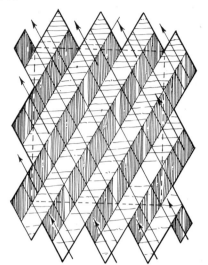

Fig. 16

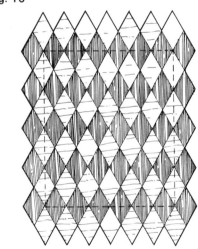

Fig. 17

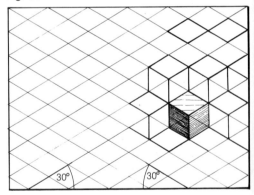

30°   30°

Fig. 14 Two sets of strips assembled.

Fig. 15 Patterns before strips are slid showing minimum size needed.

Fig. 16 Patterns showing strips after sliding into position.

Fig. 17 How cube design is drawn out.

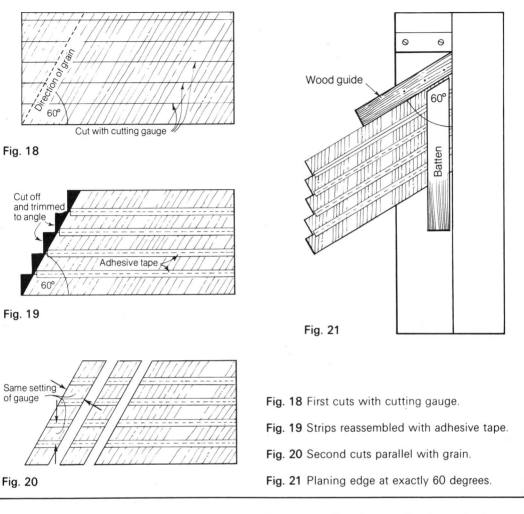

Fig. 18

Fig. 19

Fig. 20

Fig. 21

Fig. 18 First cuts with cutting gauge.

Fig. 19 Strips reassembled with adhesive tape.

Fig. 20 Second cuts parallel with grain.

Fig. 21 Planing edge at exactly 60 degrees.

he edge afresh after each cut with the gauge is made. Fig. 13 shows the two veneers with the orrect grain direction and the horizontal line of the uts to be made. They are assembled as in Fig. 14 nd sloping cuts made as shown. The assembly in ig. 15 shows the strips before being slid into osition and the minimum number of diamonds eeded for the design. Fig. 16 gives the pattern with he strips slid into position ready for trimming at the dges. It is clear that a certain amount of wastage unavoidable. Care is needed in assembling ecause the gummed tape conceals the joints.

Draw centre lines in each direction on both veneer and groundwork as a guide to laying the veneer in the correct position.

In the case of the 'cube' design Fig. 10C, although all the units are the same size and shape, it is impossible to assemble the whole in strips and slide the alternate ones as in the case of the draughts board and diamond patterns because there are no continuous straight joint lines across the whole. It is necessary to add the pieces individually or make up 'cubes' of three pieces and add them as a whole.

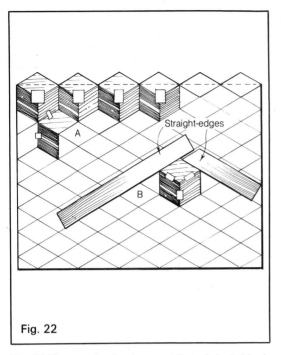

Straight-edges

A

B

Fig. 22

Fig. 22 Two methods of assembling. **A** individual pieces; **B** cubes.

All the diamonds are of the same size and shape and all have interior angles of 60deg. and 120deg. Prepare a drawing as in Fig. 17 and shade in one cube as shown to see the effect and to give the grain direction.

The best way of cutting the strips is shown in Fig. 18. After gauging and trimming they are reassembled and held with gummed tape as in Fig. 19. A cut is made at one end at 60deg. and strips cut off with the cutting gauge the same setting as before (Fig. 20). When trimming fit a wood guide to the shooting board as shown in Fig. 21. When the second batch of diamonds having the grain parallel with the edge is made, cut the end slope in the other direction, thus ensuring that the gummed tape is uppermost in all cases.

Assemble the diamonds on the drawing either individually or as complete 'cubes'. A useful guide is to fix two straight-edges in alignment with the pencil lines and fit the veneers to these as in Fig. 22. If properly prepared the diamonds will fit together accurately, but check on the drawing as the work progresses. It is a help to work horizontally down rather than to start at a corner and work diagonally across. Fig. 22 illustrates two possible methods of assembly.

Wall fitment made almost entirely from veneered
panels. Photograph by courtesy of Morris of
Glasgow.

Chapter eleven

Shaped work 1

It is in shaped work that one of the greatest advantages in veneering is apparent. There are many jobs that would be impossible without it, and others that would be unsatisfactory because of the short grain that would be inevitable, or the unsightly joints that would nesessarily show. By veneering the work can be so made that it has maximum strength and yet shows an attractive grain.

There are four main ways of making the groundwork, the choice of which depends mainly upon the design of the particular job and also upon the facilities available for doing the work. In some cases any of the methods can be adopted with success. They may be stated briefly as cutting in the solid, building up brick fashion, bending and laminating, and coopering. Fig. 1 shows at a glance the principle of the four methods. In trade workshops the laminated method is largely used; especially for mass-produced items, because the cost of the formers is spread over the entire production.

(below) Making simple shape with three veneers cramped between two formers.

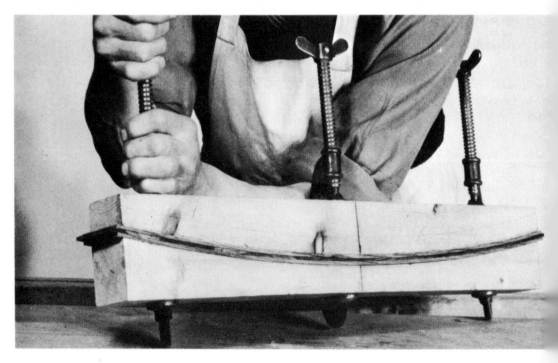

Furthermore there are ample cramping facilities. To make just one item, however, the cost of the formers might easily be prohibitive.

Cutting in the solid

It will be realized that a flat curve, such as that at Fig. 1A, could be cut in the solid and veneered with success, but it would need a thick piece of timber which would run into waste. This in a small shop might be awkward to obtain, quite apart from the difficulty of cutting. Then, supposing the curve to be more acute, as at Fig. 2A, there would be short grain at the ends which would be unsatisfactory for veneering. Generally then, cutting in the solid is suitable only for small jobs with slight curvature. When it *is* done a point to note is that the waste pieces cut away should be saved because they can usually be used for cauls.

The 'brick' method

These difficulties are largely overcome in the built-up brick method at Fig. 2B. The layers are composed of so many 'bricks' the vertical joints of which are staggered so that there is no weakness. As all the pieces are comparatively short there is no extent of end grain on the surface and no short grain. Even in an acute curve, such as that in Fig. 2, there is no difficulty, though the quicker the curve the greater the number of pieces that must be used. The method is suitable for such parts as drawer fronts, friezes, table rims, and so on.

The method of setting out the 'bricks' is shown at Fig. 3A. The required curve is drawn on a board and marks are drawn across it to show where the joints are to occur, the full lines denoting the joint of one

Fig. 1 Four methods of making shaped roundwork. A cut in solid; B laminated and bent; C built-up brick fashion; D coopered.

Fig. 2 Comparison of methods for shaped rounds. A (solid) shows a lot of end grain; (brick method) is better in this respect; laminated. End grain is entirely eliminated.

Fig. 3 How bricks are assembled for shaped work.

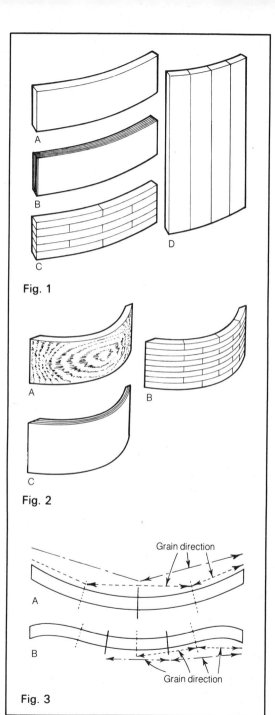

Fig. 1

Fig. 2

Fig. 3

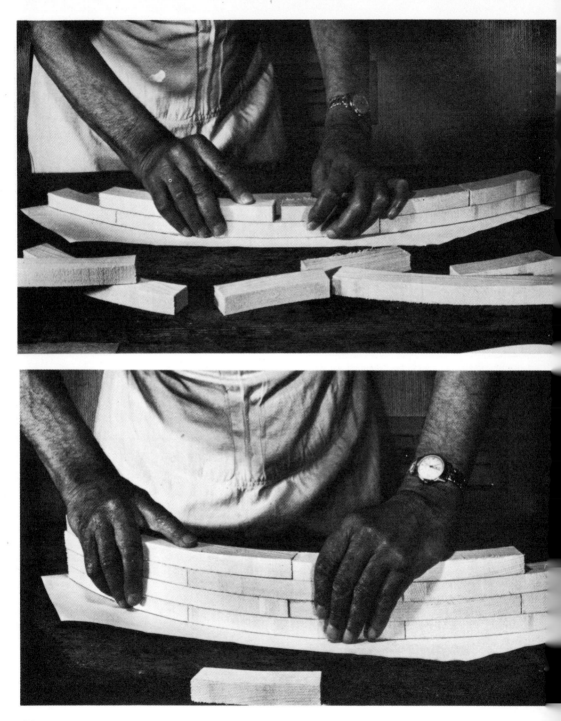

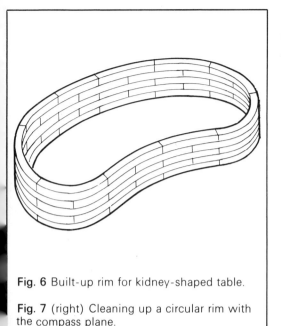

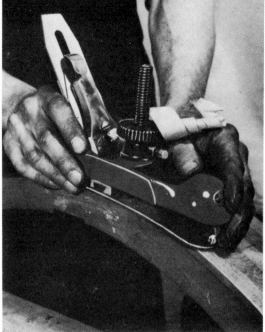

Fig. 6 Built-up rim for kidney-shaped table.

Fig. 7 (right) Cleaning up a circular rim with the compass plane.

ayer and the dotted ones those of the adjoining ones. As the curve is part of a circle only one emplate is needed for marking out, one for each ayer, and these can be cut out from plywood. If the work has to show hardwood at the edges (the top of a drawer front, for instance), two thin layers of hardwood of the complete shape can be cut out. These are useful later when gluing up because the bricks' can be assembled on them. If they are not required, the gluing up is done on the marked-out board.

he marking out is affected to an extent by whether a bandsaw is available, because the later cleaning up depends upon this. In a large shop the usual plan is to cut the bricks about 6mm. ($\frac{1}{4}$in.) extra wide at both sides (the templates being made correspondingly wide). Then, after gluing up, the whole thing is cut to the finished shape on the bandsaw. If this is not possible the bricks are cut

ig. 4 (above left) First stage in assembling bricks for shaped work.

ig. 5 (below left) Shaped rim nearly completed.

sufficiently full for cleaning up only, and are cleaned up with spokeshave or circular plane first. After gluing only a minimum of cleaning up is needed. It will be seen, then, that the facilities available have to be considered before the marking out is done.

Building up the bricks. Two stages in gluing up are shown in Fig. 4 and 5. A rubbed joint is all that is needed. After a couple of hours or so the glue will have set sufficiently for a shaving to be taken off the top so enabling the next layer to be built up. Fig. 4 shows the second layer being fitted. The work then proceeds until the total width has been assembled. If another hardwood edging is needed it can be cramped on. A similar procedure is followed in the case of work the shape of which is not part of a circle, but more templates are needed (Fig. 3B). Another instance is the kidney-shaped table rim in Fig. 6.

Cleaning up. After gluing, the surface is cleaned up with the compass plane in the case of circular curves, as in Fig. 7, or with the spokeshave. It is obviously important that the surface is perfectly

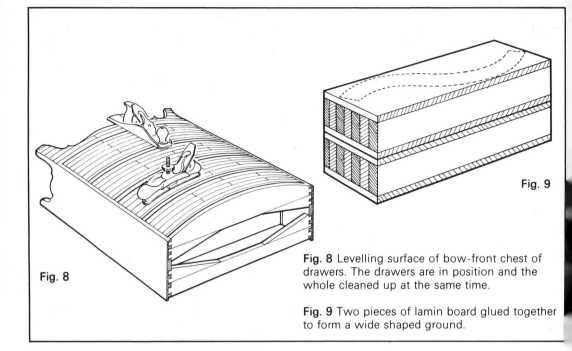

Fig. 8 Levelling surface of bow-front chest of drawers. The drawers are in position and the whole cleaned up at the same time.

Fig. 9 Two pieces of lamin board glued together to form a wide shaped ground.

flat in its width, and a useful tool to use for ensuring this is the rasp or file, this being worked sideways as well as forwards with a sliding movement so that any lumps are removed. Passing the hand lightly along the surface quickly reveals any irregularities, though it must be tested also with the straight-edge across the width. Finally a piece of the coarsest glasspaper is held round a block, the surface of which is rounded for a hollow curve or flat for a convex shape. This is worked along the surface to remove any deep file marks and to take out minor irregularities.

In some instances, of which a bow-front chest is an example, the final cleaning up is done after the drawers have been assembled and fitted in the carcase. Fig 8 shows the idea. In this way a panel plane can be passed across the whole thing, thus ensuring the entire surface being true.

Use of laminated board. It is possible in some cases to use laminated board for shaped work as in Fig. 9. Two or more pieces can be glued together to make up the thickness as shown. It makes a sort of ready built-up brick groundwork.

Bending and laminating

The tendency nowadays is to replace the bric method by the laminated method outlined below It is reckoned more reliable as there are no joints o the surface. It necessitates large heavily-buil formers upon which the wood can be bent, but fo repetition work this is economically possible. In th small shop turning out a single item, however, th cost would probably be too great and the bric method is still used. An interesting comparison o the two methods as applied to the shaped cases o a grand pianoforte is shown in Fig. 10.

Large table rims. Quite large curved table rim can be laminated, five or six thicknesses bein used. It necessitates large formers or jigs, as i Fig. 11, and, although there is a saving in the woo of the actual job, there is a great deal of waste i the former. For this reason the method is usuall undertaken only in large shops which make number of jobs to the same design, the sam former being used for all. If only one table has to b

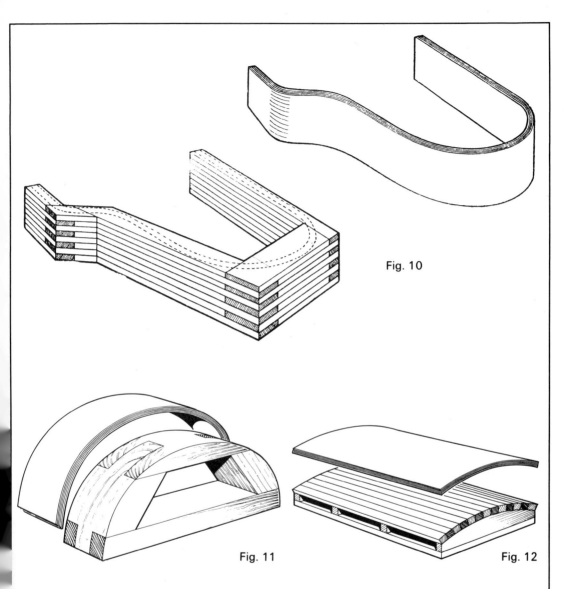

Fig. 10

Fig. 11

Fig. 12

Fig. 10 Original and modern methods of forming rim of grand piano. In the earlier built-up method the shape was bandsawn to the dotted line. Laminated rims are bent around a heavy former. It is a far less wasteful method.

Fig. 11 Large former or jig for laminating curved edging. The laminae are bent around and are cramped to the jig. Sometimes a series of holes can be bored around the side near the curve to take thumbscrews. It depends on the cramps available.

Fig. 12 Another kind of jig for assembling laminae. The strips are screwed or nailed to the cross-pieces.

made the built-up brick method is more economical and is certainly simpler. In all cases of laminating, an extra allowance should be made at both ends.

Another point is that, when several cramps are used in place of a top caul, the centre ones should always be tightened up first so that the glue is driven outwards.

Sometimes it is more convenient to make the caul of the kind shown in Fig. 12. Cross-pieces are fixed to a series of shaped members and the outer edges trimmed to the curve. For a quite simple lamination the jig shown in Fig. 13 can be made. Note the holes to enable the thumbscrews to be applied.

Occasionally a frieze or similar part is needed which is straight for most of its length and then bends at the ends. If preferred, small shaped pieces can be tongued on at the ends, but a more satisfactory way is to make one or two saw cuts according to the thickness through the width and then bend just the ends. This necessitates the ends being well steamed and cramped between shaped cauls, as in Fig. 14. It may be necessary to re-steam

and cramp again before the wood bends sufficiently. Finally, the ends are thoroughly heated, the saw kerfs glued, and a piece of saw-cut veneer placed in each kerf. After cramping down and allowing plenty of time to set, the wood will retain its shape indefinitely and can be safely veneered. Heat of course is not necessary if a cold-setting glue is used—except to accelerate setting.

Another method sometimes used for shaped parts is to glue two or more thin pieces together. A pair of cauls is needed, the shape being cut on the bandsaw from a single block. The wood is then thoroughly streamed and cramped between the cauls without glue. In very acute curves the process may need to be repeated several times before the full curve is reached. Fig 15 shows the cauls. When satisfactory the joining surfaces are glued and the whole cramped up once again. After the glue has set, the surface is cleaned up and toothed, and veneered on both sides, the same cauls being used.

Fig. 13 (below) Jig for bending laminae for narrow strips.

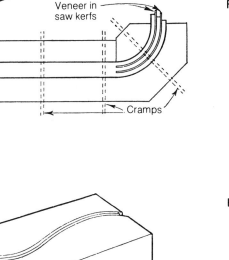

Veneer in saw kerfs

Cramps

Fig. 14

A

B

Fig. 16

Fig. 17

Fig. 15

Fig. 18

Fig. 14 Method of bending ends leaving straight centre portion. After steaming the ends are cramped in cauls. Veneers are glued in kerfs and the whole cramped again.

Fig. 15 Groundwork in two layers. These are steamed and bent between cauls without glue. When dry they are glued and cramped again.

Fig. 16 Sections through coopered doors.

Fig. 17 Cradle for building up a coopered groundwork.

Fig. 18 Shaped panel with coopered groundwork. A plywood panel is glued on at each side.

Coopering

The fourth form of groundwork is the coopered type, and the principle of this is explained in Fig. 1D. It is a form of construction used often in curved flush doors. A number of pieces are jointed together, the joints being at an angle so that the required curve can be planed. It is necessary to use extra thick stuff, as shown in Fig. 16. A convenient form of cradle on which to assemble the parts is shown in Fig. 17. If good rubbed joints are made the doors will be perfectly strong, though it is necessary to veneer both sides. Practically any shape of door can be made in this way. An example of a serpentine shape is given at Fig. 16B.

Another form of groundwork for a curved door is that shown in Fig. 18. First a cradle of the inner shape is made and a piece of ply bent around it. A series of battens about 25mm. (1in.) in section are glued on to it, and over these another sheet of ply is fixed. When the glue has set both sides are veneered. This method is successful when the curve is flat, but for a more acute shape the battens would have to be glued together and both sides planed to the curve before the plywood panels were added. Otherwise the joints would show through to the surface.

Fig. 19 Clockcase and bracket veneered with curl mahogany. For the shaped parts contact adhesive was used. Made by the author.

Chapter twelve

Shaped work 2

Although to an extent the method to be followed depends upon the particular job, it is also largely affected by the apparatus available. Large veneering shops have presses, either pneumatic or of a type capable of taking shaped formers, and these offer the simplest means. Failing these it is necessary to use shaped cauls, sandbags or sandtrays, the veneering hammer, or, for certain small work, contact adhesive. The examples in this chapter are given with alternative methods that can be followed.

Fig. 1 shows a serpentine-shaped workpiece covered with veneer, the grain of which runs crosswise. It was put down in the sandtray shown. The tray is half-filled with fine sifted sand, and the shaped groundwork pressed into it and moved back and forth so that the sand conforms to the shape. If the sand is slightly damped it will retain the shape when the groundwork is lifted. The

Fig. 1 (below) Work piece of serpentine section covered with veneer, the grain of which runs cross-wise. It rests on the sand tray in which it was put down.

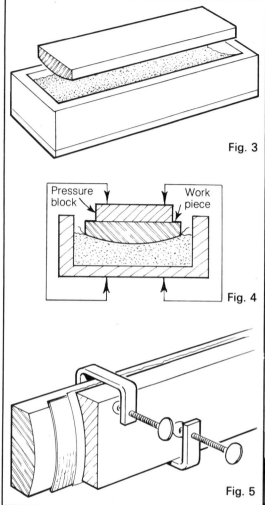

Fig. 3

Fig. 4

Fig. 2 (above) Veneered work piece cramped into sand tray.

Fig. 3 Sand box used for veneering a shaped work piece.

Fig. 4 Section through sand box showing where cramps are applied.

Fig. 5 Bowed work piece veneered with shaped caul.

latter is dried, cleaned of all sand, and both it and the veneer glued. In preference cold-setting resin glue should be used. A couple of veneer pins knocked in at the ends will prevent the veneer from shifting. Newspaper is placed over the surface and the whole carefully placed into the moulded sand. A pressure block is placed on top and the whole cramped down as in Fig. 2.

When the grain of the veneer runs lengthwise there is no difficulty in making the veneer conform to the shape of the groundwork, but if it runs crosswise as in Fig. 1 it is advisable to damp it, place it on the groundwork, and cramp into the sandtray without glue. After a few hours it can be withdrawn and it will be found to have retained approximately the shape. Unless this is done it will tend to disarrange the sand. Both it and the groundwork must be dried before glue is applied. Fig. 3 gives a rounded item raised above the sandtray, and Fig. 4 shows in section how pressure is applied.

An alternative method for this would be to use a

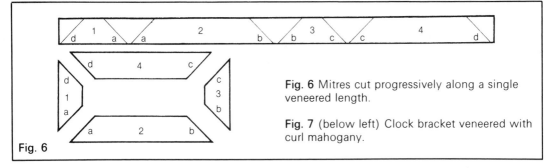

Fig. 6

Fig. 6 Mitres cut progressively along a single veneered length.

Fig. 7 (below left) Clock bracket veneered with curl mahogany.

Fig. 7

shaped caul as in Fig. 5, and if a spindle moulder is available to shape both groundwork and caul there is no difficulty. It would, however, be rather difficult to achieve an exact fit if hand methods have to be used, and several thicknesses of newspaper or a piece of felt should be interposed to even the pressure over the whole. Yet another way would be the pneumatic press or the Harefield pneumatic envelope. The latter is dealt with more fully on page 47.

In a similar class but involving a more acute bend is the dome of the clockcase on page 66. Here the groundwork was prepared in a single continuous strip, veneered, and afterwards mitred. As the groundwork was prepared by hand methods considerable care was needed to make the section constant throughout, as any discrepancy at the mitres might make it impossible to level the surface through the veneer. The best way with handwork is to cut the mitres progressively along the length as in Fig. 6. Thus A–A, B–B, etc., being close together, are bound to make a good fit. Those at D–D, of course, are a long way apart in the original length, but this cannot be avoided, and the

best way is to put this mitre at the back (though in fact in the clockcase on page 66 there was little discrepancy).

The actual laying of the veneer was done with a reverse caul long enough only to cover slightly more than the front (and back) veneer. It was thus fairly easy to make a good fit up to the groundwork, whereas a long caul to reach over all four members would be more difficult to make an exact fit, especially in the middle. In any case the veneers, being curls, had to be prepared in individual pieces. All four were put down with the same caul.

As the curve of the section was quite acute, it was necessary to stick adhesive tape over the outside to prevent cracking. The veneer was damped, cauled down without glue, and allowed to set for two or three hours when it retained its shape approximately. Afterwards both it and the groundwork were dried before glue was used. At the period when this clockcase was made only Scotch glue was available and the caul had to be heated. Today resin glue would probably be used, and no heat would be needed—except possibly to cure the glue quickly.

The clock bracket in Fig. 7 was made in a similar way but no caul was used. Instead the veneer was put down with *Thixofix* contact adhesive. It will be realized that in the lower large hollow portion the veneer itself had to be mitred as well as the groundwork. If veneered after assembling, although there would be only the thickness of the veneer difference at the narrow bottom part, at the top the divergence from the mitre would be considerable, and would be easily noticeable. Consequently the groundwork was prepared in a single length, the

Fig. 8 Parts forming the hollow member with mitres cut and front veneered ready for trimming.

mitres cut, and all three pieces veneered. When set the overhanging veneer at the mitres was trimmed flush. Fig. 8 shows the parts with the mitres cut and the surfaces veneered ready for trimming. Note the use of gummed tape to prevent the veneer from splintering.

The use of contact adhesive made the use of a caul unnecessary as the veneer would adhere immediately on touching the groundwork. First the veneer was damped, pressed without glue into the hollow, and held with a rounded block until dry. Adhesive tape was stuck to the front to prevent cracking, a coat of *Thixofix* applied to both it and the groundwork, and allowed to dry out completely. A second coat was then given and when touch-dry the veneer was held in position at the top and progressively pressed down, air being excluded. Care was necessary to work down in one direction so that the veneer did not bridge across the hollow. Ample setting time was given to ensure complete

adhesion before mitreing. The rounded portion at the top was done in much the same way, except that *Sellotape* was stuck at the front rather than gummed tape, the advantage being that it resisted damp when being temporarily bent to shape before gluing. In this case the parts were veneered first as in Fig. 9 and the mitres cut afterwards.

Bow-front panel. Shaped doors are often coopered and both front and back veneers put on simultaneously with plywood cauls as at Fig. 10A. It would be almost impossible (as well as expensive) to make shaped cauls which would fit closely up to the groundwork, and the alternative is to use plywood which will bend to shape, and fix these to shaped cross-bearers. The edges of the latter are easily cut to the required curves, and the plywood conforms to these and has sufficient strength to ensure pressure along the length. Since it is important that pressure is applied at the middle first so that surplus glue is driven towards the edges, the curvature of the cross-bearers is adjusted accordingly, that of the top bearers being slightly flatter than the finished curve, and that of the bottom ones slightly quicker as at Fig. 10B.

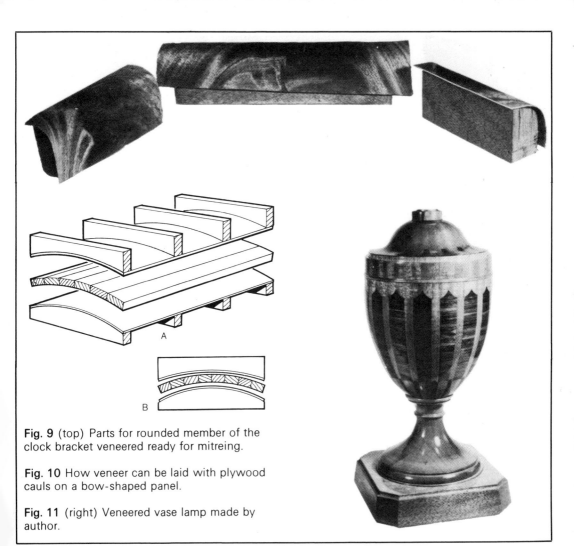

Fig. 9 (top) Parts for rounded member of the clock bracket veneered ready for mitreing.

Fig. 10 How veneer can be laid with plywood cauls on a bow-shaped panel.

Fig. 11 (right) Veneered vase lamp made by author.

Both should be increased or decreased by the same amount. If the plywood is too stiff to bend easily it should be cramped down to a curve beforehand and left for as long as possible, so that it sets to a curve. It is nailed to the top and bottom cross-bearers. Cramps are applied to the ends of the latter and pressure is thus felt at the middle first.

A second advantage of the method is that no cramps are necessary at the middle of the cross-bearers where it would be difficult to reach. Cold-setting resin glue is advisable because it would be difficult to heat the plywood cauls sufficiently to melt animal glue. In fact, if the latter were essential it would be advisable to use zinc sheets beneath the plywood as these would retain the heat for a longer period. In any case assistance would be almost imperative to enable the whole process to be completed before the cauls became chilled. (See also the alternative method on page 99).

Vase lamp. Another example of a coopered groundwork is the electric lamp in Fig. 11, designed in the form of a late eighteenth century urn or vase.

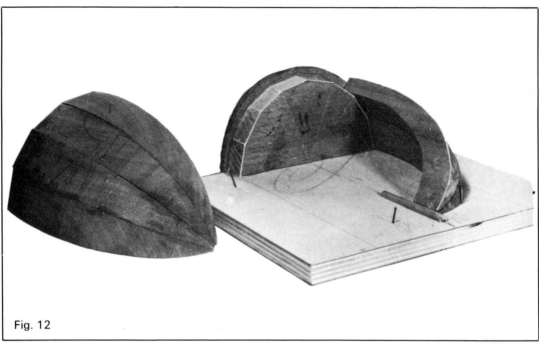

Fig. 12

Fig. 14

Fig. 15

Fig. 12 (above opposite) Cradle used for assembling the staves of the urn shown in Fig. 11.

Fig. 13 (below opposite) Shaped caul used to press down the strips of veneer. The lathe forms a convenient means of holding the workpiece.

Fig. 14 (above left) The urn veneered and awaiting final cleaning up.

Fig. 15 (top right) Veneers for the lid being tailored to shape and held with gummed tape.

Fig. 16 (bottom right) Veneers for the lid pressed down with a caul held with centre bolt and fly nut.

Fig. 16

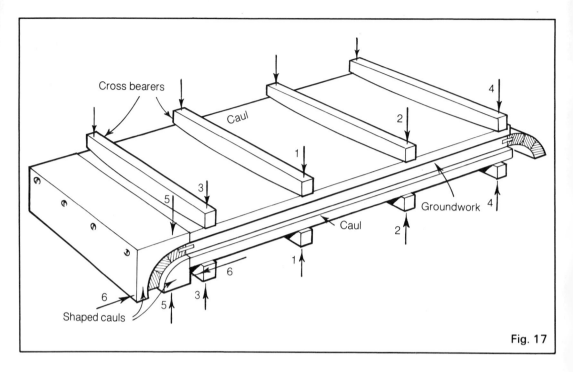

Cross bearers

Caul

Groundwork

Shaped cauls

Caul

Fig. 17

The staves forming the shape were assembled first in pairs on a cradle as in Fig. 12, each pair then being glued together, until finally two complete halves were formed. These were planed to a true fit with each other, and glue-rubbed together. After turning to shape, the veneer strips were put down individually. To avoid crumbling the outer sides of the strips were covered with gummed tape, and the shapes marked out from a template and cut with the knife. Afterwards the ends were trimmed to the line on the shooting board. As the wide strips were cross-grained it was necessary to make a caul to press down, this being shaped both in length and across the width to conform to the compound shape. This was heated and cramped down as shown in Fig. 13, Scotch glue being used. After about two hours the caul was removed and the squeezed-out glue at the edges scraped away.

Done in this way it was easy to fit the narrow, long-grained strips between the others since, owing to the tapered shape, they could be slid in and rubbed down with the cross-peen of the hammer. Gummed tape was stuck over all joints, this being peeled off after the glue had set, slight

damping helping the process. The scraper was used for cleaning up and finally the urn was revolved in the lathe at the lowest speed and finished with No. $1\frac{1}{2}$ glasspaper followed by Flour grade. Fig. 14 has the urn before final cleaning up.

In the case of the lid the veneers had to be tailored to fit the shape and were held together with pieces of gummed tape as in Fig. 15. All were put down in a single operation with a reverse caul turned in the lathe. To ensure a close fit for the caul a template was used for testing, but the final fit was by holding a strip of coarse glasspaper across the lid and pressing it against the revolving caul. As the glass-paper was approximately the same thickness as the veneer the fit was really close. Cramping was with a bolt passed through the centre as in Fig. 16.

Shaped corners. The panel shown in Fig. 17 is an example of work requiring either shaped solid cauls or sandbags. It would not be practicable to use the hammer—at any rate if the grain of the veneer is across the curve.

The method of forming the shaped corners depends

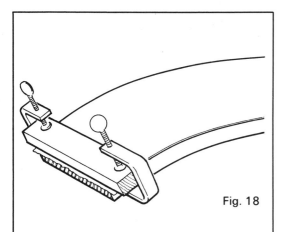

Fig. 18

Fig. 17 Caul veneering a flat panel with shaped ends. The inner edges of the cross-bearers are slightly curved. Note order in which cramps are applied.

Fig. 18 End of veneer cramped to prevent springing.

mainly upon the size of the curve. In some cases a single block could be fixed on, the section being arranged to enable the shape to be worked in it. Usually, however, it is necessary to build it up cooper-fashion as shown. Three strips are usually sufficient, the thickness being arranged so that they will hold up the curve. They are rub-jointed on a cradle and when dry are fixed to the centre panel with a loose tongue joint as shown. This means that cramping is necessary, and to enable the cramps to be applied blocks must be glued on temporarily. When dry they are knocked off and the shaping completed. The main flat groundwork is of lamin board.

Bending the veneers. As the curves are fairly acute it is advisable to bend the veneer before laying. This is done by fixing flat cauls at each side as in Fig. 17 the length of these being arranged so that they line up exactly at the point where the curve begins. Two pairs of shaped cauls are also needed. The ends of the veneer are damped and the flat cauls fixed down. The shaped cauls are then heated and cramped on. If left on for two or three hours the veneer will retain the curve after

the cauls are removed. Before removing them about four screws should be driven in to enter the top caul as shown. These are to prevent it from slipping down when the final cramping is being done. The holes should be extra large to allow for a certain amount of adjustment.

When gluing down it is essential that the glue is driven from the centre outwards. Consequently the flat cauls must be pressed down first and the cross-bearers must be slightly curved at the inner edge as in Fig. 17. For the same reason when the shaped cauls are pressed the handscrews operating vertically (5) are put on first and the others (6) put on afterwards. Otherwise the glue is liable to be driven upwards from the ends and be unable to escape.

After gluing both veneer and groundwork drive in one or two veneer pins in the flat part to prevent the veneer from floating. Heat the cauls thoroughly if Scotch glue is used and place them so that their ends line up with the start of the curve (Fig. 17).

Fix down the cross-bearers, starting with the middle ones first. Assistance is really essential so that the opposite screws can be tightened simultaneously.

The top shaped caul is placed in position and the screws driven in with a moderate tightness. The lower caul is then placed in position and the vertical cramp (5) put on. Immediately afterwards the horizontal cramp (6) can be tightened. It will be appreciated that speed in the operation is essential when Scotch glue is used because the cauls are liable to lose their heat quickly. A cold-setting glue such as resin gives more time for the operation.

In a workshop in which a spindle is available it is a simple matter to make the pairs of cauls to the exact shape. If they are made by hand a sheet of felt should be placed beneath so that the pressure is equalized in the event of any unevenness.

In the case of a shaped edge the veneer can usually be rubbed down with the cross-peen of the hammer. The mirror frame shown on page 64 is an example. When the curve is very acute the veneer can be damped and held round a dowel rod with a rubber band. When dry it will retain its shape and not be liable to spring up.

Fig. 19 Large curved plywood panels for dressing table fronts, bonded with Aerolite KL, are quickly cured in the press by means of low-voltage heating at the factory of F. Wrighton & Sons Ltd. Photograph by courtesy of CIBA (A.R.L.) Ltd.

Sometimes when veneer is laid by the hammer around a curve the ends tend to spring up. This can be prevented by cramping a wood strip at the end with newspaper interposed as in Fig. 18.

Chapter thirteen

Inlay strings and bandings

Strictly speaking, this subject scarcely comes under the heading of veneering, because bandings are used as often in solid work as in conjuction with veneer. There is something akin to veneering, however, in that bandings are in reality a form of veneer.

There is a wide range of patterns of ready-made strings and bandings that can be used to decorate furniture, and it is scarcely worth while making them up by hand unless a special pattern is required or 'unless it is required to match an existing design which is not a stock pattern. The thickness is usually in the region of 1 mm. ($\frac{1}{25}$in.) in the bandings. Strings (which are single lines of inlay) can be obtained in similar thicknesses and varying widths, or in square sections. The latter form are especially useful for inlaying at edges, where they are seen both from above and at the side.

In a machine shop the groove or rebate, as the case may be, to hold the inlay is cut on the spindle, but in handwork the scratch-stock is used for all small inlays and all those set in from the edge. For wide bandings fitted at the edge of, say, a table-top, the rebate is more conveniently cut with a rebate plane. In fitting square lines at the edge a cutting gauge can be used, this being worked first at the top and then at the side.

The scratch-stock. The tool used chiefly is the scratch-stock a home-made appliance. Its form can be varied slightly, but that shown in Fig. 1 has all the essentials. Actual sizes are unimportant, but it is advisable not to make its total thickness too great, as it then becomes somewhat clumsy. When making it, two pieces of hardwood are screwed together and the notch marked out and cut in both. Done in this way the two pieces always go together in exactly the same positions. When required for use around a hollow shape, a second scratch is necessary, the upright notch of which is rounded so that there is only one point of contact against the edge of the work. The horizontal edge should be slightly rounded in any case so that at the start of the cut the tool can be tilted forward to help the cut.

(left) Wine cabinet veneered with burr walnut. Photograph by courtesy of Waring & Gillow Ltd.

The cutter can conveniently be filed up from a piece of old saw blade. The width is approximately that of the inlay banding, though this is ascertained by trial on a spare piece of wood. The actual cutting edge is filed perfectly square so that it cuts both on the forward and backward stroke. It is held in the main stock by tightening the screws. Occasionally it is necessary to withdraw one of the screws entirely to enable the cutter to be placed in a position where it would otherwise foul the screw.

In use, the scratch-stock is held with the notch pressed tightly against the edge of the wood, and is worked back and forth with a downward pressure as in Fig. 2. In this way a groove is gradually formed, the depth of which is the same

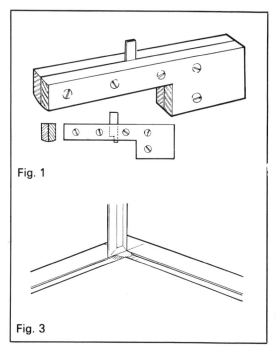

Fig. 1

Fig. 3

Fig. 1 Details of the scratch-stock. Length could be about 15cm. (6in.).

Fig. 2 (below) Using scratch-stock to work groove for inlay string.

Fig. 3 Use of chisel to cut in corners of inlay groove

throughout, since the scratch automatically ceases to cut when a depth equal to the projection of the cutter has been formed. Incidentally, it may be noted that this projection should be a trifle less than the thickness of the inlay, so that pressure can be applied to the inlay when the latter is laid. If the groove is too deep, the pressure will be exerted on the surrounding wood instead of on the inlay, resulting in a little gap under the inlay, a most undesirable feature.

It is obviously necessary to keep the scratch pressed tightly against the work, but, apart from this, there is little difficulty when working *with* the grain. When cross-grain has to be negotiated it is sometimes desirable to cut across first with the cutting gauge, both sides being so cut. This prevents the grain from splintering out. Care must be taken at corners not to overrun. The best plan is to work the scratch-stock in both directions up to a safe distance and mark the corners with pencil. A chisel can be used, as in Fig. 3 the waste being

Fig. 4 (below) Inlay banding being pressed down with cross—peen of hammer.

eased away, with a narrow chisel after which the scratch-stock can be worked right up to the corners. When any extent of inlaying across the grain has to be done, a special cutter can be filed up in which a small projecting nicker is made at each side so that the grain is cut before the waste is scratched away.

When the inlay is right at the edge it is important to hold the scratch-stock well down on the surface at the completion of the operation because if it tilts it will cut an uneven rebate. For this reason many prefer to gauge in both width and thickness and remove the waste with the rebate plane.

Gluing down the bandings. When Scotch glue is used it is desirable to work fairly rapidly when gluing down to avoid chilling the glue. For this reason it should be done in a warm shop free from draughts. Put glue both in the groove and on the inlay, and place the latter quickly in position at one end, holding the other end up and feeding it into the groove. The cross-peen of a hammer is used to press the inlay down, as shown in Fig. 4. It is here that the desirability of the inlay standing up slightly

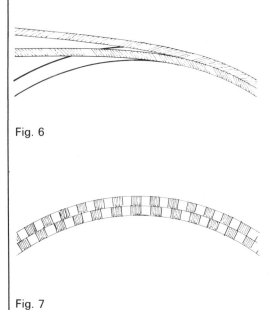

Fig. 6

Fig. 7

Fig. 8

Fig. 5 (top) Mitreing banding with chisel.

Fig. 6 Herringbone banding separated to fit around curve.

Fig. 7 Unbalanced effect, the result of separating banding of regular pattern.

Fig. 8 How inlay string can be held at edge with string passed around nails.

Fig. 9 Inlay string held at edge with rubber bands passed around nails driven into rebate.

is realized. If the groove is too deep the hammer presses on the wood at the sides of the groove. When a gap is left under the inlay the glue shrinks in time and pulls the inlay down with it, leaving an unsightly depression.

Other glues, resin or P.V.A., can be used but as they have not the tackiness of Scotch glue the groove should be of a width to grip the inlay, as otherwise the latter may tend to spring up. As these are used cold no heating is necessary.

Mitred corners. In most cases the corners are mitred. The best plan is to fit all mitres before gluing, cutting the joints with a chisel as in Fig. 5. If the inlay is a fairly tight fit it will remain down without any difficulty. If it should spring, a caul can be handscrewed down over it with a piece of paper between. It is most important that plenty of time is allowed for the glue to harden—twenty-four hours at least, and more if possible.

When a banding has to be laid round an acute curve it is usually necessary to make up a special piece of banding to fit. For flatter curves, however, it is usually sufficient to separate the parts of the banding (unless the banding is very narrow or the curve very flat). Fig. 6 shows a herring-bone banding separated to make it sufficiently pliable. It should be noted that this cannot be done if certain regular patterns of inlay are used, because, when separated and bent, the one tends to slide along the other owing to the larger radius it has to negotiate. This results in an unbalanced pattern, as in Fig. 7.

A difficulty that sometimes occurs is that of holding down a string at an edge owing to a tendency for it to spring. Fig. 8 shows how this can be overcome by handscrewing a batten at each side near the edge. Nails are driven into these at intervals, enabling string to be passed from nail to nail, as shown. When the string is damped it pulls the inlay tightly home. The same method can be followed when inlaying a string around a curved edge. Fig. 9 shows an inlaid string held in position with elastic bands fitted over nails driven into the rebate of the frame.

115

Fig. 10 Scratch-stock with double fence used for tapered leg in moulding box.

For inlaying lines in turned, tapered, or other forms of legs, the apparatus in Fig. 10 is useful. The scratch-stock is worked along the side of the box.

It is usually desirable to make a scratch-stock with double fence as shown as it prevents the tool from shifting laterally.

Sometimes it may be required to inlay a line to a curved shape independently of an edge, and clearly the scratch-stock could not be used. Generally, the simplest way of working the groove to receive it is to cut a template of the shape preferably in metal and use a tool such as a narrow chisel or a bradawl working this against the curved template.

Generally it is advisable to mark first in pencil as otherwise it is difficult to know where to start and stop the groove. If the curve is extra acute, it may be necessary to steam the inlay line first, bend to approximate shape, and leave to dry out before gluing in position.

Chapter fourteen

Adhesives

The introduction and development of modern adhesives has largely revolutionized the methods used in laying veneers—at any rate as far as large-scale factory production is concerned. Although more expensive than the traditional animal and casein glues, they have many advantages. Apart from being extremely strong and highly damp- and heat-proof, they have the great manufacturing advantage that they can be heat-cured, so that a machine is freed for more work in a matter of seconds. This is an obvious gain to the manufacturer who specializes in veneering only, since the plant need never remain idle. However, the older adhesives still have their uses and in some cases have their advantages. American trade names for adhesives are included in brackets.

Synthetic resin. In the trade various types are used, some hot application, others cold, but for the most part the latter is used for veneering and is heat-cured. For the smaller user a cold urea-formaldehyde type resin (Poly-urethane) is the most suitable. It can be used for most veneering jobs, but its most obvious advantage is for table tops and similar work in that it is both heat- and water-resistant, and makes so strong a bond that a solid lipping at the edges is not needed. It calls for careful application, however, because once cured it cannot be re-liquefied. An even spread of glue is important because if there is an accumulation in any part which the caul or press fails to even out it cannot be corrected once it has set. Bubbles in the veneer caused by the parts being glue-starved or possibly because of irregularities in the caul failing to press down the veneer evenly, can generally be corrected by making a thin cut with a knife through the veneer and introducing fresh glue, but it is better to avoid even this. A machine glue spreader is the ideal means of applying the adhesive (see page 46), but failing this a toothed applicator such as that on page 55, or a roller, should be used after the initial coating with a brush. No time should be lost in evening out the coating because, although there is reasonable time for assembly, setting begins as soon as the glue is mixed. It is not like animal glue which can be (and often is) left for a while before pressing takes place.

Fig. 1 (left) Extending table with rosewood veneered top. Courtesy Heal & Son. Ltd.

One such glue is *Aerolite 300 (Boat Armor Epoxy Resin)* used with a powder hardener *L48*. The glue itself is a fairly thick syrup which remains usable for several months, but begins to set as soon as the hardener is added. For the man needing the glue only occasionally its limited shelf life may be a disadvantage, and a more suitable glue is *Aerolite 306 (Boat Armor Epoxy Resin)* which is in powder form and has a much longer shelf life. It requires only the addition of water when it becomes the syrup *300*, needing only the addition of the hardener.

Incidentally, in general woodwork the separate-application method is common, the glue being applied to one part of a joint and liquid hardener to the other. This is not practicable in veneering because the application of a liquid hardener to the veneer would cause it to buckle—especially some difficult woods. To mix the liquid hardener with the syrup might cause too rapid setting, but the addition of the powder hardener is quite successful.

Another resin is *Cascamite (Secur-It or Tight-Bond)* waterproof glue. This is in powder form and has the hardener already incorporated, requiring only the addition of water. It has a long shelf life if the container is kept sealed, and should be applied evenly as described.

All resin glues require either a press or cauls for veneering. The hammer method cannot be used. Only sufficient pressure is needed to ensure that the veneer is brought into close and even contact with the groundwork, otherwise the bond may be glue-starved by excessive pressure. It follows then that the groundwork must be really flat so that the press or caul bears evenly over the entire surface. In shaped work the accurate fitting of a reverse caul is essential.

As already mentioned, heat is used to accelerate setting in trade workshops, presses being used in which either hot water is circulated through the platens to give heat, or the whole thing passes through a heating chamber. Alternatively R.F. (radio frequency) heating may be used. Curing by heat when cauls are used is scarcely practicable, however, because it is doubtful whether there would be time to complete the adjustment of all the cramps before setting occurs.

Polyvinyl-acetate (PVA) *(Poly-urethane).* Many PVA glues contain resin additives and although they are more widely used in general assembly work, they can be used for veneering—at any rate for small work. For large areas it may be difficult to obtain an even spread as the assembly time is fairly short before an initial set takes place. The glue requires no preparation but consists of a white cream needing only to be applied cold from the container. The hammer method cannot be used.

Casein. This is in powder form requiring only the addition of water. It can be used for veneering, but has the disadvantage of being liable to stain veneers. Great care has to be taken not to allow any glue to be on the surface of the veneer otherwise darkening inevitably takes place. Even so penetration through the grain may take place, and glue exuding through joints can cause trouble. A so-called non-staining type can be obtained but it is in fact not entirely free from staining. Casein is applied cold and either press or cauls are needed. The hammer method is impracticable.

Animal glue. More generally known as Scotch glue, this is the traditional glue of the cabinet maker. It has considerable strength when properly used but is neither heat- nor water-proof. Press, caul, or hammer method can be used, but heat is needed to liquefy the glue after the veneer is in position. Careful preparation of the glue is essential. It can be obtained in cake or pearl form, the former requiring to be broken up into usable size in sacking. It is placed in the container, covered with cold water, and left overnight. A water-heated kettle is used for heating the container the next day, and the mixture stirred until the water has been absorbed. The glue should never be boiled, but should be heated to a rather greater temperature than can be borne by the hand. When the brush is lifted a few inches from the pot the glue should run down freely without lumps yet without breaking up into drops.

Fig. 2 (above right) Wall furniture veneered with curl mahogany. Courtesy of E. Gomme Ltd.

Fig. 3 (below right) Boat-shaped table veneered with rosewood. Courtesy Heal & Son Ltd.

Fig. 4 Veneered chess-board table. By courtesy of Waring and Gillow Ltd.

It is the only glue that can be used with the hammer method (see Chapter seven), but it can be used equally well for press or caul veneering. For these, of course, heat is essential, and in winter time it is desirable to defer the work until the afternoon when the workshop has had time to warm up. Otherwise the cauls may be chilled before they have had time to liquefy the glue. A proprietary animal glue is *Croid Universal* (*Contact cement*) which can be used for hammer, caul, or press veneering. It is put up in tins and needs to be heated by the usual methods to enable the veneer to be pressed down flat.

Contact adhesives. although these are not suitable for large areas, they are useful for small-scale jobs, especially shaped work (see page 103). Since the two parts, veneer and groundwork, immediately grab on being brought into contact with each other no caul is needed, an obvious advantage in shaped work. At the same time great care is needed to see that every part of the veneer is in close contact with the groundwork, and this in shaped work means working progressively around the curve so that no air is trapped and there are no bubbles. Experience has shown that the best results are obtained by double coating both veneer and groundwork. The first coat on both is left to dry out completely. After the application of the second coat the adhesive is allowed to become touch-dry (about 15 minutes) before the veneer is placed in position. A point to remember is that the two parts grab immediately on being brought into contact. Careful positioning of the veneer is therefore essential. Adhesives of the contact type are *Thixofix* and *Evo-stick 5655*, (*Epoxy*) both of which can be brush-applied, though it is an advantage to follow with a hand spreader with serrated edge (page 55). Some contact adhesives are too thick to give an even spread and begin to gel too quickly for ridges of adhesive to be evened out.

Glue film. In this the adhesive is in the form of a thin tissue with paper backing. It is cut to the required size and placed face downwards on the groundwork. It is heated with either the flat iron set to its lowest heat or heated in front of the fire when

Fig. 5 Conference table in Macassar ebony, the matched veneers of the top in radial pattern.

Designed by Martin Hall MSIA. Courtesy of Gordon Russell Ltd.

the paper backing can be peeled off. The veneer is now placed in position and the paper backing put on top. Bonding is completed either by cramping a heated caul over the whole or using the flat iron as above and pressing down. Any tendency for the veneer to rise can be corrected by using either a roller or the veneering hammer. It will be realized that the adhesive is not heat proof and is therefore not the ideal for table tops on which hot items may be stood.

Special adhesives. Sometimes in marquetry work materials such as brass, tortoise shell, ivory, etc., are included, but the general run of adhesives can be used; UF resin, freshly made Scotch glue, etc. However, in repair work it is sometimes necessary to refix inlay of brass which have lifted. An excellent adhesive for this is epoxy resin glue such as *Araldite* (*Epoxy*). This is a two-part glue normally put up in tubes, the two parts remaining plastic until mixed with each other, when setting begins; when hard it forms a strong bond. Usually it is necessary to cramp a flat block over the repair with newspaper interposed until setting is complete.

Fig. 6 Dining table designed by Desmond Ryan. The interlocking sections are made from cylinders of silver-anodised metal, in-filled with orange-stained veneer circles on plywood backing.

Index